INSIGHT POCKET GUIDE

KUALA

C000174109

APA PUBLICATIONS
Part of the Langenscheidt Publishing Group

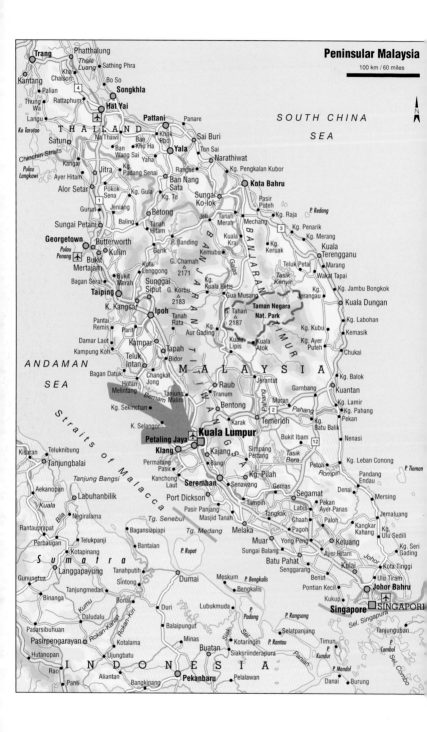

introduction

Welcome

This guidebook combines the interests and enthusiasms of two of the world's best-known information providers: Insight Guides, who have set the standard for visual travel guides since 1970, and Discovery Channel, the world's premier source of non-fiction television programming. Its aim is to bring you the best of Kuala Lumpur and its surroundings in a series of tailor-made itineraries devised by Insight's Malaysia correspondent, Shoba Devan.

The capital of Malaysia, Kuala Lumpur was a run-down shanty town on the edge of a marshy riverbank some 100 years ago. Today, this former mining outpost has transformed itself into a burgeoning multicultural city of two million, with a skyline that boasts the tallest buildings in the world. The first three full-day itineraries string together the most essential sights of KL (as its inhabitants fondly refer to it), from the historic heart of the city to Chinatown and the leafy Lake Gardens. These are followed by a series of optional tours which cover sights as diverse as Kampung Bahru, KL's Malay quarter; the Hindu cave temple at Batu Caves; and the bustling mega-malls of Bukit Bintang. For visitors with more time, there are excursions to remote islands, lush rainforests and highland resorts. Chapters on shopping, eating out and nightlife, plus a practical information section covering travel essentials complete this reader-friendly guide.

Shoba Devan moved her base to Kuala Lumpur in 1982 out of sheer necessity. But as she became familiar with the city's smells, sounds and sights, she looked beyond the concrete skyscrapers and saw a certain rusticity about it. Despite its apparent modernity, the city has retained a certain idyllic charm. For Devan, KL's small-town hospitality manifests itself subtly – the smile of recognition from the neighbourhood soya bean milk hawker; the spirited political discussions of the local barber; and the hammy performances of sidewalk medicine men. Devan hopes this book will unleash the explorer in you and lead you to discover what really makes Kuala Lumpur tick.

6   **contents**

Preceding pages: the Moorish-inspired Sultan Abdul Samad Building
Following pages: festive National Day Parade

History & Culture

Kuala Lumpur was never the centre of an ancient culture or civilisation. No philosopher, scientist or general can lay claim to its inspiration. Indeed, just 100 years ago, it was nothing more than marsh, muck and mudbank.

In 1857, an expedition of Chinese tin miners headed up the Klang River from Peng Kalan Batu (now Port Klang), then the capital of the Sultanate of Selangor in Malaya. They were prospecting for tin, a mineral that commanded the kind of attention that is reserved for oil these days. After several days, they arrived at the confluence of the Klang and Gombak rivers, where they had to stop as the rivers were too shallow to accommodate their fully-laden flotilla. Their resting place was nothing more than a tiny hamlet nestled in a quagmire of mud. Appropriately, the miners called the place Kuala Lumpur – literally meaning 'muddy confluence'.

Tin was eventually found in Ampang, upstream of Kuala Lumpur, but because the rivers were shallow, direct access to the mines was limited. Thus, Kuala Lumpur became a convenient staging point for supplies and ore to be brought in or sent out. Buoyed by high tin prices, Kuala Lumpur developed into a flourishing village by the 1860s. Chinese labourers were imported by the thousands to operate the mines that had opened up its hinterland. There were some Malays – mainly Bugis traders from Celebes – but the Chinese immigrants began to dominate. Soon, Kuala Lumpur took on the veneer of a booming mining town – with seedy brothels, gambling dens and organised crime.

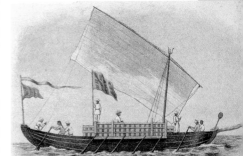

Self-governance

The aristocrats of Selangor at first did not interfere with this development. They were content to collect export duties from the mined ore, and left the control of the Chinese immigrants largely in the hands of a community leader called the 'Kapitan China'. The most illustrious Kapitan was Yap Ah Loy. A Hakka immigrant who came to the country when he was only 17, Yap's tenure of office from 1868 till 1885 proved significant in the development of Kuala Lumpur.

Gradually, Kuala Lumpur grew in prominence. In 1867, Selangor was torn by civil war; the bone of contention being the right to collect export duties on tin. Initially, the war focused on gaining control of the forts sited at the river estuaries where the Malay royalty was based. The miners of Kuala Lumpur, fearing the war, shipped their ore through whatever river route was open to them. However, as duties from tin slowly dwindled in the ports, the warring parties moved into Kuala Lumpur.

Left: 19th century street scene in Kuala Lumpur
Right: a Malayan *prahu* (boat) dating back to the 1880s

Meanwhile, Yap Ah Loy allied himself with Tengku Kudin, the Viceroy of Selangor. His enemies were led by Syed Hashor, a determined and resourceful man who enlisted the help of other Malay chiefs and overran Kuala Lumpur in August 1872, razing it to the ground. In 1873, Tengku Kudin, with the help of Malay forces from Pahang, regained the town.

Yap Ah Loy is credited with ensuring that Kuala Lumpur did not disappear back into the marsh. After the war, with the town ruined and tin prices low, the Chinese immigrants were ready to pack up and leave. Yap, however, borrowed capital to redevelop Kuala Lumpur and cajoled the immigrants to stay to inspire confidence. Five years later, the strategy paid off as tin prices soared. In 1879, for the first time, a British official was stationed in Kuala Lumpur and in 1880, Selangor moved its capital to Kuala Lumpur.

Modernisation

The next major personality in the city's history was Frank Swettenham, the Resident of Selangor appointed in 1882. Swettenham replaced the shanties and huts that formed much of Kuala Lumpur with brick structures. He was also responsible for the construction of the Kuala Lumpur–Klang railway link, ending the city's dependence on the river.

The city continued to grow. An active policy of emigration, the setting aside of reserves, and the encouragement of agriculture on its periphery increased the Malay population while diminishing the economic stronghold of the Chinese migrants. Indian labourers were brought in to work on coffee and rubber estates and on the railroad. The city became more cosmopolitan.

In 1896, Kuala Lumpur was declared the capital of the Federated Malay States. Both world wars did little damage to the city, and in 1957, 100 years

history/culture

after the first mining expedition, the campsite was finally deemed worthy as the capital of sovereign Malaya. In 1963, Kuala Lumpur became the capital of Malaysia, and in 1972, it gained city status. Significantly, the city was also wrenched from Selangor and declared a Federal Territory in 1974, similar to the status enjoyed by Washington's District of Columbia. Since then the city has bloomed into one of the fastest growing in Southeast Asia. However, in some areas, basic infrastructure has not kept pace with the city's unbridled growth. The traffic jams, pollution and crowded streets are evidence of this.

In recent years, KL, as the city is known, has been erecting massive new buildings as a symbol of its aspirations to be a proud capital, not merely of Malaysia, but the world. These skyscrapers are seen as embodiments of the country's aim to be the spokesperson of Southeast Asia in global dialogues from trade and finance to information technology and international security. These and other national mega-projects, a good selection of which are found in the capital, are funded largely by foreign borrowings, something which has not been overly helpful to the country's debt levels.

However, KL's impressive skyline and its modern structures do give it the feel of an international city. Some visitors like this, since they can, fairly effortlessly, find enough global stamps of familiarity to be able to take to the city easily. From fast-food outlets and hotel chains to shopping malls and department stores, international brand names and products abound, at least superficially so; occasionally, some aspects are tempered with local quirkiness, such as spicy Indian curry pizzas and four-star accommodation without the requisite 24-hour room service.

On the other hand, visitors expecting an ancient city untainted by Western norms, and with traditional architectural heritage intact, are likely to be disappointed with the modernity of KL. There are, however, pockets of the old KL – the ones that every city, no matter how modern, still possesses. So you might come across a colourful Hindu temple at a busy junction, or a row of pre-war shophouses behind a mall, while the sound of squawking chickens could well lead you to a wet market that has existed for generations. However, these finds might serve only to reinforce how rapidly the erosion of unique traditions has occurred, and will continue to occur, as KL and Malaysia seek to find a foothold in an era of globalisation.

Luckily, the city's more contemporary structures of glass and steel conveniently appeal to enough camera-happy visitors to make tourism one of the city's biggest revenue-earners. In fact, buildings like Petronas Twin Towers – the world's tallest buildings currently – are gradually taking precedence over the traditional tourism attractions that date back to colonial times.

Top left: Frank Swettenham, the Resident of Selangor
Left: most early Chinese migrants worked as labourers
Right: Kuala Lumpur's Petronas Twin Towers

A Melting Pot

Visitors to Kuala Lumpur will be fascinated by its obvious multi-culturalism: predominantly Malays, with smaller groups of Chinese, Indians, Eurasians, Portuguese and many people of mixed races. At one time, the city was divided along racial lines, with members of a race dominating an entire neighbourhood. These days, racially diverse neighbourhoods are more common.

Still, certain areas remain the stronghold of one dominant race. The Chinese occupy Chinatown of course, and much of the nearby Pudu, Sungai Besi and Salak South areas. They are mainly Cantonese, though a fair number of Hokkiens live there as well. Most of the Chinese population are adher-

ents of the traditional Taoist and Buddhist faiths, though a substantial number have adopted Christianity.

The Malays have tended to congregate in the Kampung Bahru, Datuk Keramat, Ulu Kelang, Ampang and Sungai Pencala areas. Many still have *kampung* or village roots outside the city, but this is slowly changing. All are Muslims (to renounce Islam is a crime punishable by the law), hence the profusion of mosques, particularly in Malay neighbourhoods. However, liberalism is practised, and tolerance towards other religions has grown beyond mere lip service to the constitutional right to freedom of faith for other races. This is physically manifested in the presence of places of worship of other religious denominations, even in the capital's Malay heart of Kampung Bahru.

The Indian neighbourhoods are mainly in the Jalan Tun Sambanthan and Sentul areas. Their presence here is related to the fact that Malayan Railways once maintained housing for their labourers in these areas. Most of the Indians were from South India, but a fair sprinkling of Northerners – notably Punjabis, Sindhis and Gujeratis – also came to Kuala Lumpur for business. Sri Lankan Tamils were also brought over by the colonial authorities as administrative and clerical staff. Indians are mainly Hindu, though there is a very prominent Indian-Muslim community in Kuala Lumpur.

Nonetheless, racial harmony is very much in evidence. Sober-suited Chinese and Malay businessmen sweat out a curry lunch at an Indian restaurant. Uniform jeans-and-T-shirt-clad youth of indeterminate racial origin hang out at the malls. Weekends find nightclubs filled with slinkily-dressed, trendy 20- and 30-somethings, gyrating to American R&B or Chilean Latin grooves, even while some in the group might abstain from alcohol or beef for religious purposes. And at the annual City Day Big Walk, folk from all backgrounds turn out in their track suits or shorts to put their best leg forward for health and a good cause.

The kaleidoscopic nature of Kuala Lumpur society has given rise to a host of social and religious norms, some of which apply to only one community and others to all. It is traditional, for instance, to remove your shoes before entering the homes of Malays, Indians and Chinese. Pointing your foot

Above: multi-culturalism is a unique aspect of the city **Top right:** soccer-mad Malaysian youths **Right:** Masjid Jamek Mosque is an important place of worship

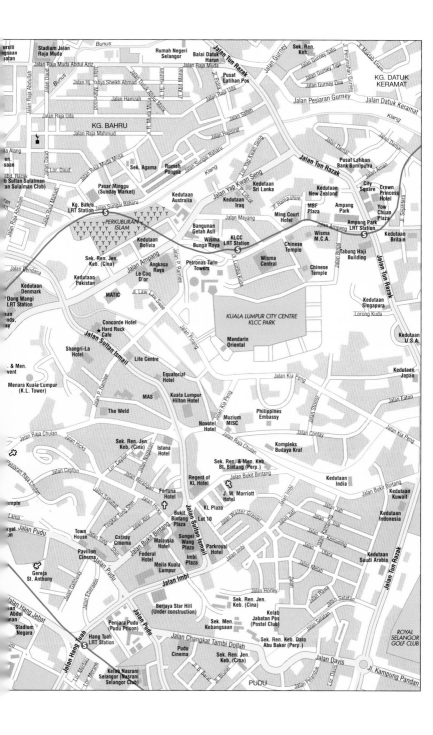

City Itineraries

city itineraries

he first three days in Kuala Lumpur should be allocated to orienting yourself to this cosmopolitan city. The first day allows you to appreciate Kuala
Lumpur's historic origins; the second, its present role as a thriving
marketplace; and the third, to reflect upon its quieter, greener areas.

The unrelenting pace of construction is what still gives Kuala Lumpur (KL)
the feel of a booming city despite being over 150 years old. Much of the
new development concentrates on flyovers and the much-awaited public rail
transport system. Massive redevelopment projects include the Kuala Lumpur
City Centre (KLCC) in the heart of the prestigious Golden Triangle, the financial and commercial district. The Petronas Twin Towers are only the
first of a host of other structures being planned in that area.

The half-day itineraries, focusing on both the city as well as its immediate surroundings, are a guide to KL's different faces and cater to various
interests. KL wears a different face during the day from the night, and while
the itineraries include a suggestion of best times to visit, it is sometimes
worthwhile going back to the same place in the evening. The city assumes
a different aura again during festivities, particularly its various ethnic hubs
to which the festivals are pertinent, for instance, Kampung Bahru during
the Muslim Hari Raya, and Chinatown during Chinese New Year.

While the itineraries highlight the main attractions, various nooks and cran-
nies nearby can reveal interesting insights on KL life. It is generally safe
to give in to your exploratory instincts during the day, although the usual
commonsense safety rules apply. The curious and friendly KL-ite would
be happy to help out anyone who gets lost.

Hot-footing It

Most of KL's attractions are accessible by foot, though pedestrian walkways
were obviously not a priority on the modern town builders' agendas. Heavy
traffic and pollution do not help. Nonetheless, walking is the quickest way
to get around during gridlock rush hours, and especially when it rains. Therefore, if possible, avoid road transport between 7–9am and 4–7pm on weekdays, and 1–2pm on Saturdays. For those not used to the humidity, start the
half-day itineraries early and aim to finish up between 11am–3pm.

To travel between attractions, hop into a taxi, or the air-conditioned
Light Rail Transport System (LRT) or KTM Komuter electric trains.
For a real local experience, try the buses during peak hours. Trains
and buses also bring you out to KL's outer attractions. Alternatively,
negotiate to book a taxi for the day. Many of these places are also
part of guided tours from KL. The recommended excursions
provide more rural experiences, includ-
ing tropical greenery in recreational
parks and forests, and village life.

Left: the Sultan Abdul Samad building
Right: a schoolgirl with national flag

1. GETTING ACQUAINTED *(see map below)*

Breakfast and a walk around Market Square; lunch at the hawker stalls; linger at the historic hub, then stroll to the Railway Station. End the day with dinner at the Central Market.

Starting point is Medan Pasar Lama, behind Central Market, close to the Pasar Seni LRT stop

This tour is designed to give you a feel of the city, from its origins as a colonial outpost to the thriving metropolis it is today. Start with a breakfast of steamed (yes, steamed) bread and *kaya* (a delicious jam of coconut and eggs) at the **Sin Seng Nam Restaurant** at **Medan Pasar Lama**. The square is one of the oldest parts of the city, its Georgio-Romanesque facades resplendent, if somewhat incongruous with its surroundings, in the morning sun. This is where the city's first brick buildings were erected.

After breakfast, walk down the square towards the 12-storey Hong Kong Bank Building (opposite the Bank of Tokyo) and turn left. You are now at **Benteng**, and can clearly see the confluence of two rivers – the Gombak and Klang – that gives the city its name. Head along Benteng

Above: Dataran Merdeka is the city's historic centre

till you reach Jalan Tun Perak, then turn left and cross the bridge. In front of the Masjid Jamek LRT Station and on your left you will find the entrance to **Masjid Jamek** (Jame Mosque), a sprawl of colonnades and spires around a peaceful square. This beautiful building is the city's oldest mosque.

Moorish Influence

Further down, on the same side of the street, you will come to the city's most regal neighbourhood, despite the thrust of the LRT line. Done in Moorish majesty, these blocks of colonial buildings around the **Padang** (Green) comprise the historical heart of Kuala Lumpur city. This is where the British administrators of the Federated Malay States built their headquarters in the 1890s. For some reason, the colonial architects of the Public Works Department deemed the Moghul style of architecture appropriate for the government buildings of the Malay Peninsula. The distinct style is completely imported from another British outpost, India. The building facing Jalan Tun Perak houses the **Sessions and Magistrates Courts**.

Turn left at the junction with Jalan Raja and continue down past the bridge. Here, in the shade, petition writers hold sway. On the left is the former colonial administrative centre, the **Bangunan Sultan Abdul Samad**, now the Supreme Court, and one of the most photographed of the city's landmarks. Come back again at night to see this magnificent building lit up; it is a pretty sight indeed. The road in front of this building, Jalan Raja, is off limits to traffic on Saturday nights when youngsters, lovers, and families hang out here or stroll along the road, enjoying the night breeze and bright lights.

Jalan Raja and the Padang are also the focus of annual Hari Merdeka (Independence Day) parades on 31 August. Colourfully-costumed KL-ites, including school bands and corporate representatives, strut their stuff in a display of national pride.

Directly opposite the Bangunan Sultan Abdul Samad across the Padang is a cluster of Tudor-style buildings. This is another colonial relic, the members-only **Royal Selangor Club** (circa 1884), which prides itself on an ambience that dates back to the days when Somerset Maugham was a regular visitor.

The massive plaza to the left of the Padang is the **Dataran Merdeka** (Independence Square), anchored by one of the world's tallest flagpoles and a giant video screen. Underground is a shopping arcade with entertainment outlets and restaurants. This is also the home to The Actor's Studio, one of the busiest performing venues in town, with its two theatres. Around the Padang are several other colonial buildings which have been restored and turned into museums, notably the National Museum (Muzium Negara) and the Kuala Lumpur Memorial Library.

There are two options from here. Across the busy Jalan Kinabalu on Jalan Tangsi is another colonial gem dating back to 1907. The **PAM Building**

Right: fountain detail at Dataran Merdeka

hosts the Persaturan Arkitek Malaysia (Architect's Association of Malaysia). You might want to cool off with a beer at the pub here. Back at the Padang facing the Bangunan Sultan Abdul Samad, a quiet little church sits on the far left, **St Mary's Cathedral**, which was built in the Gothic tradition in 1894. Services are still held here.

Back across Jalan Raja is **Muzium Tekstil** (Textile Museum; tel: 291 7136; open daily 9.30am–6pm). This museum caters to textile enthusiasts, researchers and neophytes alike. Wander through the adjacent Museum Shoppe which carries various Malaysian paraphernalia, including textiles, woodcarvings and pottery.

For a quiet, relaxing lunch, try the hawker stalls behind the Muzium Tekstil, which offer a variety of spicy Malay meat and vegetable dishes to go with rice, making for decent budget meals.

Islamic Influences

Head back to Jalan Raja, and veer left. You will come to the gleaming white **Menara Dayabumi** (Dayabumi Complex), with its fine filigree-like Islamic design. It is at its most impressive at night when it is floodlit. Go past the **General Post Office** (POS 2020; open Mon–Fri 7.30am–5pm, Sat 7.30am–2pm, closed Sun), and take the pedestrian subway to the other side of Jalan Sultan Hishamuddin. Ahead is the **Masjid Negara** (National Mosque; open Sat–Thurs 9am–6pm, Fri 3–6pm) with its 73-m (240-ft) tall minaret and geometric lattice-work. Resplendent in white marble offset by pools of gurgling water, the National Mosque accommodates up to 10,000 people at a time. If you wish to enter the mosque, remove your shoes and use the robe provided if you are wearing shorts. Tour the interior to see the ornamental pools, fountains, a gallery, the library and the Grand Prayer Hall. Tourists, however, are forbidden from entering the Prayer Hall.

The last of the Moghul-style buildings to be constructed, the **Bangunan KTM Berhad** (Railway Administration Building), down the road from the mosque, is architecturally stunning. Another Moorish architecture extravagance, the **Stesen Keretapi Kuala Lumpur** (Kuala Lumpur Railway

Station) stands opposite, and can be accessed by an underground pass beneath the busy road. The building is part of the city's proud efforts at architectural preservation. First completed in 1885, it was rebuilt at the turn of the century. It was subsequently extensively renovated in the 1980s and equipped with modern facilities, including a tourist information centre and restaurants. The **Heritage Station Hotel** within it offers accommodation in an old-world setting. On the top floor of the station are backpackers accommodations – The Travellers Station – with nice views.

Walk through the railway station to get to Jalan Cheng Lock. From Platform 1, head left until you reach a subway and head for the exit on Platform 4. Occasionally, late at night, the famous and very expensive cream-and-white Eastern and Oriental Express (see *Practical Information*) train passes through on its way from either Singapore or Bangkok. On a much more mundane level, the KTM Komuter trains head out from Platforms 2, 2A and 3 to Port Klang, Seremban and Rawang.

Hand-made Goodies

You will now be facing **Jalan Cheng Lock**. Turn left and walk some 500m (546yds) to the landmark **Central Market** (Pasar Seni). Once the city's largest wet produce market, this was converted in the late 1980s into a cultural-cum-shopping mall. Its art deco features and its high ceilings were renovated and repainted recently. This is a great place to shop for souvenirs. A good variety of goods are sold here, including handicrafts, souvenirs and art, all at fairly reasonable prices. Be sure to bargain for your purchases though. Regular evening cultural performances are held at the riverside amphitheatre. Pick up a brochure here or at the tourist office, and you may be lucky enough to catch a music, dance or shadow puppet performance for free.

Just outside, a pedestrian mall fronts quaint old shops selling dried fish, rice wine and Taoist icons. At the back is another row of pre-war buildings turned souvenir shops and restaurants. Central Market is a popular hangout for Malay youth, particularly boys and young men. It is not rare to see guitarists among them, testament to the fact that this was the birthplace of the local underground music scene, comprising mainly rock bands whose hole-in-the-knee and faded jeans-clad members are known locally as *Mat Rock*.

For dinner, head for the **Riverbank** (tel: 227 36652) at the Central Market for modestly priced Western and local food and beers. There are also tables outside, great for people-watching if you don't mind the humidity.

Left: a lasting British legacy is the KL Railway Station **Top:** traditional Malaysian *wau bulan* (moon kite) **Right:** a Chinese painter at Central Market

2. CHINATOWN *(see map, p27)*

Visit a money museum; walk down atmospheric Petaling Street; have a Chinese vegetarian lunch; visit Hindu and Chinese temples; and end the evening with an open-air seafood dinner.

Starting point is the Muzium Numismatik in the Menara Maybank tower, close to the Puduraya Bus and Taxi Station

Chinatown in Kuala Lumpur is similar to Chinatowns everywhere in the world (except perhaps China) – a colourful collage of earthy people, colourful temples and shops, and noisy restaurants.

Start the day by visiting a money museum, the **Muzium Numismatik** or Numismatic Museum (open daily 10am–6pm), located in the rear lobby

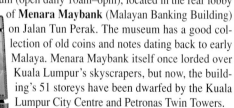

of **Menara Maybank** (Malayan Banking Building) on Jalan Tun Perak. The museum has a good collection of old coins and notes dating back to early Malaya. Menara Maybank itself once lorded over Kuala Lumpur's skyscrapers, but now, the building's 51 storeys have been dwarfed by the Kuala Lumpur City Centre and Petronas Twin Towers.

On the other side of the roundabout in front of the money museum is Chinatown. Use the zebra crossing to get over to the Sinar Kota Shopping Complex. Ahead is one of the craziest traffic-choked roundabouts in the city, on the other side of which is the Puduraya Bus and Taxi Station – long-distance buses and taxis leave from here for destinations throughout the peninsula, Singapore and Thailand. There are small hotels in the building itself and close by, convenient for late night arrivals or early morning departures. Walk along the Sinar Kota building as it turns right into **Jalan Cheng Lock**. Alternatively, you may want to shop in the large Metrojaya department store inside. Cross the road at

Top: deity at Persatuan Kwong Siew Chinese Temple
Above: mooncakes are sold only during Lantern Festival in September

the traffic light into **Jalan Sultan**. Ahead sprawls Kuala Lumpur's China-town district.

Chinatown is concentrated in Jalan Petaling, Jalan Tun H S Lee and Jalan Hang Lekir. It is usually referred to as Petaling Street, the main thoroughfare of which is cordoned off for a popular night market from 6pm to midnight. Typical of Chinatowns, there are medicine shops with jars of dried roots and herbs, and other products of less salubrious origins. There are sidewalk palm readers and fortune tellers perched on stools and whose 'tools' are laid out in open briefcases. There are tea houses and art shops, coffin makers and hidden temples, pet shops and flower vendors. A large number of stores sell cheap clothing, and backpacker accommodation is plentiful here too; Chinatown is definitely a focus for tourists.

Fascinating Facets

Interestingly, the character of Chinatown changes through the day. In the morning, people throng *dim sum* restaurants for breakfast and the wet market is active with housewives picking at the fresh produce. In the afternoon, there is a lull, but come evening, numerous stalls selling food and merchandise are set up in preparation for the after-office hours crowd. As darkness falls, and particularly on weekends, Chinatown's atmosphere is almost electric. City folk and tourists are drawn to bargains in the night market, or to sample the excellent food by the roadside or on the 'five-foot-way' (the local term for a shaded footpath). And well into the wee hours of the morning, long after most stall-owners have packed up, late-nighters, some bleary-eyed from night-clubbing, have their suppers under the bright flourescent lights of a few late-night stalls. For this reason, you may want to start this tour in the afternoon instead, so that you can experience nightfall here.

From Jalan Sultan, head past the Rex Cinema and turn right into **Jalan Hang Lekir**, lined with shops selling dried pork floss and other Chinese delicacies. Stop at one of the many Chinese restaurants at the Jalan Petaling intersection and have a typical Chinese breakfast. There are any number of noodle dishes to try out, including soupy rice noodles or the soya sauce base *kon loh* style. You could also have a go at *pau*, Chinese dumplings with meat or bean paste fillings, or *bak-kut-teh*, a fragrant stew of pork ribs and herbs. Food in Chinatown is usually not *halal* and therefore taboo for Muslims.

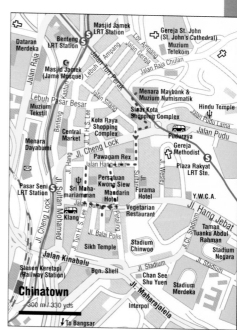

Something for Everyone

Just down the street, Jalan Hang Lekir meets Jalan Petaling. The latter is not just chaotic; it is pure anarchy. Here, sidewalk vendors and pedestrians compete with cars negotiating the narrow road. Shopping here is an exciting, even heady experience but some people find it exhausting. This is also delightful fodder for the camera-happy, but photographers would do well to ask permission before taking photos as many people object.

There are a couple of things you should know about shopping in Chinatown. First, to get the best price, bargain enthusiastically. Second, despite whatever you are told, it is not the place for designer labels. You may see vendors hawking Gucci handbags and Cartier watches which look uncannily like the real thing.

To get to your lunch spot, walk down Jalan Petaling towards Jalan Sultan. Turn right at Jalan Sultan and after about 50m (165ft), turn left into a small alley called **Jalan Panggung**, just before the Ocean Supermarket. Walk down another 50m (165ft) and you will reach **Wan Fo Yuan Vegetarian Restaurant** where you can try a reasonably-priced Chinese vegetarian meal. Chinese vegetarian cooking is an art form in its own right. The food is made to resemble meat or fish (and sometimes even tastes like the real McCoy) but is made entirely from soya bean gluten.

After lunch, turn right and head back towards Jalan Sultan, where you turn left and walk towards the junction with **Jalan Tun H S Lee**. Turn right at this junction and you will see the **Sri Mahamariamman Hindu Temple** (open daily 8am–6pm) on the left side of the road. The temple is an arresting sight, all the more for its incongruent Chinese setting. Built in 1873, the temple occupies an important place in Hindu religious life, as it is from here that the annual Thaipusam pilgrimage to Batu Caves (*see Itinerary 7*) begins. Remove your footwear first if you decide to enter the temple. Outside, vendors sell fragrant jasmine flowers strung into garlands. Buy one, drape it around your neck, and let its fragrance revitalise you.

Further down on the right side of the road is **Persatuan Kwong Siew Chinese Temple** (open daily 7am–5pm), built by the Kwong Siew Association in 1888. Watch the devotees make incense offerings, but watch discreetly and be especially mindful of when and of whom you photograph. There is usually a donation box and a nominal donation is generally appreciated.

After this, continue your shopping spree, or return to your hotel if your legs don't feel up to it.

Above: a Chinese favourite – grilled dried pork slices
Right: gateway to Sri Mahamariamman Hindu Temple

3. LAKE GARDENS AND THE NATIONAL MUSEUM
(see map, p30)

A Malay breakfast; morning stroll around Lake Gardens, visiting its deer, bird and butterfly parks, and hibiscus and orchid gardens; a spicy Indian lunch eaten off banana leaves; National Museum; dinner at an open-air hawker centre.

Starting point is a back entrance to the Lake Gardens on Jalan Cenderasi, accessible from the National Mosque. The closest KTM Komuter train station is the Kuala Lumpur Sentral Station; taxis are plentiful here

Alfred Venning, the former British State Treasurer, was more interested in the idea of creating a paradisiacal botanical garden amid lakes in the heart of Kuala Lumpur than with making money. Now, 100 years later, the name Venning scarcely means anything to most KL-ites, but his legacy strikes deep in the heart of the city. The **Lake Gardens** (Taman Tasik Perdana; open Mon–Sat 10am–6pm, Sun and public holidays 8am–6pm), with its 104ha (257 acres) of close-cropped lawns, undulating hills and carefully cultivated gardens, is a sanctuary from the maddening mayhem of the city. The leafy Lake Gardens is also a valuable green lung, helping to cleanse the city of its polluted air.

Start the day early, with a typical local breakfast on the fringes of the Lake Gardens. Tell the taxi driver to take you to Jalan Cenderasi, on the left and off Jalan Sultan Hishamuddin after the National Mosque. Get off in front of the Tanglin Clinic. Directly opposite, under the shade of rain trees, is a stall selling *nasi lemak*, a typical Malaysian breakfast meal of fragrant rice cooked in coconut milk with side dishes like *ikan bilis sambal* (anchovies cooked with chillies), *rendang* (beef cooked with spices and coconut milk), peanuts and cucumber. The stall is closed on Sunday.

Apart from the gardens, there are other attractions in the area, including the Deer Park with several local species, even the smallest species in the world, the mousedeer; Bird Park, one of the region's largest aviaries; Butterfly Park, a sanctuary for some 6,000 winged creatures; Orchid Garden and

city itineraries

Hibiscus Garden, with hundreds of luxuriant blooms; and the quirky **Dinosaur Park**, where plants are pruned into dinosaur shapes.

You won't have time to visit all the parks in a few hours so take this suggested route. After breakfast, walk 200m (660ft) up the road to the **Butterfly Park** (open daily 9am–6pm). Continue to the **Hibiscus Garden** (open daily 9am–6pm), a 10-minute walk up Jalan Cenderawasih, where it meets Jalan Tembusu. Then follow the signs to the **Bird Park** (open daily 9am–5pm) and the **Orchid Garden** (open daily 9am–6pm). The nearby **Tun Razak's Memorial** is a tribute to Malaysia's second Prime Minister. Retrace your path to the **Deer Park** (open daily 9am–6pm), which children especially find delightful. Instead of walking, you may prefer to use the park's shuttle bus (operates daily 9am–6.15pm with a break at lunchtime).

After a relaxing morning, backtrack to Jalan Cenderawasih and keep walking until you reach Jalan Parlimen. The **Tugu Kebangsaan** (National Monument) is just opposite Jalan Parlimen and contains fine sculptures and bronzework. The adjacent **ASEAN Sculpture Garden** features sculptures from the region (ASEAN is a regional economic and political association comprising Singapore, Malaysia, Indonesia, Brunei, the Philippines, Thailand, Myanmar, Laos, Cambodia and Vietnam).

Spicy Lunch

As it will be lunchtime, take a taxi to **Brickfields**, just 2km (1¼ miles) or a 10-minute ride away. Try a typical South Indian lunch, eaten off a banana

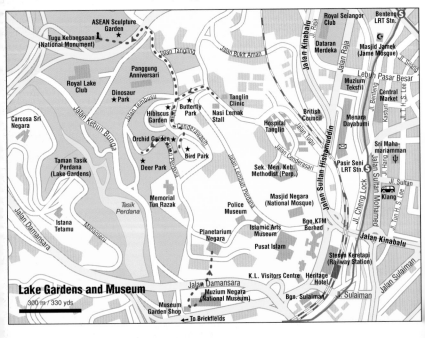

leaf, at the **Sri Devi Restaurant** on Jalan Travers (tel: 227 44173). Ask for either steamed plain rice, *beryani* (fragrant basmati rice), or *thosai* (rice flour-based pancakes). There is a variety of side dishes to accompany the meal. Lentil gravy and vegetables come with the rice or *thosai,* and the spicy, dry-fried mutton is highly recommended. In true South Indian style, the meal is eaten with the fingers of the right hand only, but ask for cutlery if you wish. Wash the meal down with a glass of cold *lassi,* a yoghurt-based drink. To end the meal, indulge in sweets like *jelebi, mysore pak* or *ladu,* but dieters be warned that these are loaded with sugar and milk.

From Brickfields, take a taxi to the **Muzium Negara** (National Museum; open daily 9am–6pm) where you can spend a couple of hours soaking up Malaysian history, local culture, and arts and craft. Of note are its social and cultural sections; these include a section on the Nonyas and Babas, the unique fusion of Chinese and Malay races. The museum features some off-beat exhibits – such as cats and treasures from dug-up graves, and the skull of an elephant which is said to have derailed a train in Malaysia – all thanks to its former curator, Datuk Sharum Yub.

The museum is small enough not to require a guided tour, so wander from room to room on your own. Its extensive reference library is also accessible to the public with permission from the curator. The building itself is of interest, influenced by the old Malay *kampung* (village) house, and topped by the 'buffalo-horned' Minangkabau-style roof. Two massive Italian glass murals are its other distinct features. Within the grounds there is a charming **Museum Garden Shop**, which is worth visiting for its local and Asian handicrafts, including coconut-craft and ceramics.

A pedestrian bridge behind the museum leads to the **Planetarium Negara** (National Planetarium; tel: 227 35484; open Sat–Thurs 10am–4.15pm). However, if the gate is closed, there is a pathway across a little further down Jalan Damansara. The planetarium has a 36-cm (14-inch) telescope and a theatre. It also houses the Arianne IV space engine that was used to launch Malaysia's first satellite, the Measat I. Its well-designed garden is scattered with replicas of ancient observatories.

International-ville

For dinner, take a taxi to the **Bangsar Seafood Village** (tel: 282 2555) along Jalan Telawi Empat in Bangsar. The speciality here is Chinese-style seafood. Try the abalone with mushroom and shrimp, or ask the waiter about the catch of the day. The yam basket and sizzling *tofu* on hotplate are also recommended.

After your meal, take a walk around Bangsar, the city's definitive area for KL's trendy. Lined with wall-to-wall pubs, coffeehouses and beautiful people, this is also a popular hangout for expatriates. There is also a wide range of international restaurants, and the alley of open-air Indian and Malay stalls, called the Bangsar stalls, are crowded from the time they set up shop at dinnertime till the early hours of the morning.

Top left: Bird Park's flamingos
Right: the National Monument

4. BUKIT BINTANG *(see map below)*

Browse at Kompleks Budaya Kraf; a Maritime Museum; shopping and strolling along Bukit Bintang before tucking into a wholesome Chinese porridge supper.

Starting point is Kompleks Budaya Kraf on Jalan Conlay off Jalan Raja Chulan. To get there, take a taxi from the KLCC LRT Station

This tour is a journey through Kuala Lumpur's mall strip in the city's most prestigious commercial area, the 'Golden Triangle'. This tour is recommended as an evening itinerary, but start earlier if you enjoy shopping. You can also use this tour to locate the shops you want to return to later.

Begin at Jalan Conlay at the **Kompleks Budaya Kraf** (open daily 10am–6pm). This 'one-stop craft centre' – a more upmarket version of the Central Market – showcases quality Malaysian arts and crafts and houses commercial bazaars, a souvenir shop, a DIY batik corner, restaurant, and the Craft Museum. Souvenir hunters will have a field day here. In one corner of the complex is the Artists' Colony, where many up and coming Malaysian artists can be seen honing their skills.

Head up Jalan Conlay to Jalan Raja Chulan. On your left, amongst the trees you will see the **Seri Melayu Restaurant** (tel: 245 1833). You will also see **Eden Seafood Village** (tel: 241 4027) across the road. Both serve good Malaysian food and offer nightly entertainment. Just at the junction is the **Muzium MISC** (open Mon–Fri 9am–4.15pm, Sat 9am–12.15pm), located on the ground floor. The museum is devoted to maritime exhibits with a good display of model boats, traditional craft, safety equipment and accounts of great maritime explorers. When finished, turn left and head to the Jalan Bukit Bintang intersection, where you should be extra careful when crossing the busy road.

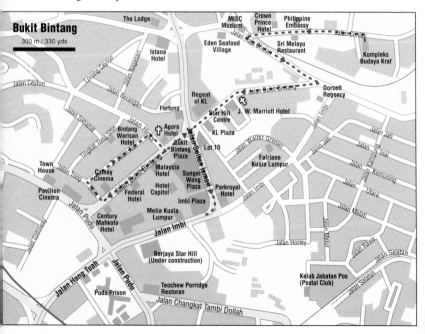

This is the beginning of **Jalan Bukit Bintang**, Kuala Lumpur's most established shopping street, which has been injected with 'mod' thanks to a recent facelift. A wide pedestrian walkway goes all the way up the road, which is lined with international open-air cafés, ice-creameries, malls and restaurants. This is a great place to watch Kuala Lumpur's trendy. The stretch begins about 500m (546 yds) from the intersection, where you see the JW Marriott Hotel and **Star Hill/CK Tangs** on the left. Opposite is the **Regent of Kuala Lumpur**, with its classy decor, considered one of the city's leading hotels. Star Hill houses CK Tangs, a Singaporean-owned department store, and exclusive designer boutiques.

Shops, shops, and more shops

Continuing on, you come to **Kuala Lumpur Plaza**, a four-storey shopping extravaganza, with the country's largest music store, the American chain Tower Records, as its anchor tenant. Right next to Kuala Lumpur Plaza is **Lot 10**, a fashionable hangout that has, in addition to upmarket shops and the Japanese-owned Isetan Department Store, numerous chic restaurants and coffee joints where the city's hip crowds like to hang out.

Across the street from the flashy Lot 10 is **Sungei Wang Plaza** (which you will visit later) and **Bukit Bintang Plaza**, both about 20m (65ft) left of the traffic lights and boasting large department stores. Sungei Wang's anchor tenant is Parkson Grand, while the upmarket Metrojaya dominates the Bukit Bintang Plaza. The real strength of these stores or, for that matter, most of the stores in this area, is clothing, from *haute couture* designer togs to the more moderately-priced Malaysian-made apparel. In addition, there is no lack of shoes, belts, handbags, wallets and other leather accessories. Metrojaya, Tangs and Isetan also have a good range of imported cosmetics and toiletries. Tip: although cosmetics in Malaysia are duty free, prices at these stores are probably still lower than those found at so-called duty-free stores.

Bukit Bintang's offerings also encompass a whole lot of other goods, from watches and cameras to photographic equipment and books. The prices are reasonable as the area is popular with locals and competition among retailers is stiff. Sungei Wang, in particular, can get very crowded, especially during major festival periods. Several times during the year, goods are marked down by as much as 70 percent, and, in the third quarter of the year, the whole street gets dressed up for a major shopping carnival.

Above: Lot 10 is a popular hangout for the hip
Right: a shopping day at Bukit Bintang

From Bukit Bintang Plaza, turn left at the main entrance and head down Jalan Bukit Bintang. This section houses hotels and a modern upmarket open-air hawker centre, where you can have wine with your food, and be serenaded by local bands.

Local Eats

Keep walking and some 500m (546yds) further down, you will come to the Federal Hotel. Then cross the road to the Cathay Cinema. Head down behind the cinema and you are in **Jalan Alor**. Behind placid shopfronts and sani-

tised fast-food outlets lurks another personality – one that comes out with the stars. The first sign of this is the bright neons and tell-tale red lights that seem to spring up from every second storey window. Jalan Alor transforms itself from a congested city street into brightly lit chaos of food stalls selling a whole range of Chinese cuisine, from the mundane to the exotic – venison, tripe and seafood – for prices beginning at under RM5. At the end of the road at the Jalan Hicks junction, turn right, and you are back in Jalan Bukit Bintang.

Cross the road and turn left until you reach a set of traffic lights. At the junction, turn right and head down **Jalan Sultan Ismail**. Keep to the right side of the road. At the traffic lights past Sungei Wang Plaza, turn right into Jalan Imbi. You will now be approaching **Imbi Plaza**, which backs Sungei Wang Plaza.

Imbi Plaza is Kuala Lumpur's computer mall, where you can get bargain basement prices for clones, peripherals and software, including games.

Bird's Eye-view

If you have time, take a taxi to **Menara Kuala Lumpur** (open daily 10am–10pm) for a vertigo-inducing view of the city from the top of one of the world's tallest buildings. This Islamic-influenced tower also has a souvenir shop, revolving restaurant and the world's highest MacDonalds. If you are peckish, grab a taxi back to Bukit Bintang to Jalan Pudu. On the junction of Jalan Pudu and Jalan Imbi is **Pudu Prison**, built in 1895, and once housing the country's most notorious criminals. It is now awaiting redevelopment, although a small section might be retained as a museum. The mural on its wall makes up the world's longest painting. The **Teochew Porridge Restoran** (tel: 248 3452; open daily 7am–3pm and 6pm–4am) at 270 Jalan Changkat Tambi Dollah, off Jalan Pudu, specialises in, as the shop's name says, Teochew porridge, a rice broth served with meat, fried fish and preserved vegetables. The restaurant also serves very popular *dim sum*.

Above: night lights at Bukit Bintang

5. KAMPUNG BAHRU WALK *(see map, p36)*

A tour of the oldest Malay settlement; visit a Sikh temple and a mosque; and a browse through a Malay bazaar.

Starting point is Jalan Raja Alang in Kampung Bahru. You can take a taxi there from the Sultan Ismail or Dang Wangi LRT stations

This tour takes you around the oldest Malay settlement in Kuala Lumpur – **Kampung Bahru**, literally translates to 'New Village', and has its roots in the early 19th century influx of Malay settlers to Kuala Lumpur. Though it is not new – the settlement was established in 1899 – this short walk reveals an oasis of peaceful community living typical of rural Malay villages, somehow successfully ignoring the surrounding frenetic urbanisation. Start this tour in the late evening for glimpses of neighbours catching up after work and children playing. The Muslim fasting month of Ramadan is a particularly good time to do this tour. Head here just before the break of fast at sunset, when the streets are a riot of food stalls, and you get to sample delicacies cooked only during this period.

Head down **Jalan Raja Alang** from its junction with **Jalan Tuanku Abdul Rahman**. The road is supposedly for vehicular traffic, but often the crowds spill over the sidewalks and onto the road. As you walk down Jalan Raja Alang, try some fruit from the stalls on the left. In addition to apples, oranges and bananas, some specialise in exotic tropical fruits that rarely see the light of a supermarket shelf. Depending on the season, you might find durian, mangosteen, rambutan, guava and jackfruit, among others. Further down, there is a municipal hawker food emporium, **Pusat Penjaja Dewan Bandaraya**, where good Malay food is served. Try the *mee jawa* or *mee sop*, both noodle-based dishes, for breakfast, before continuing your journey.

One would have thought that a Sikh temple would be out of place in a largely Muslim neighbourhood. The red-bricked **Kampung Bahru Sikh Temple** further down the road from Pusat Penjaja Dewan Bandaraya, is yet another testament to the cultural and religious tolerance practised by

Above: a Kampung Bahru fruit vendor

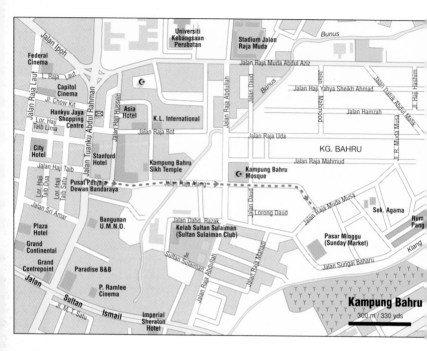

Malaysians. The facade of the temple is reminiscent of KL's pre-war shop-houses. The gates are normally closed to traffic, but there is a side entrance that allows individuals to enter. In consonance with the Sikh faith, there are no icons inside. Instead, pictures of Sikh saints line the entrance hall. The temple is open only occasionally and during special festivals, so you may have to make do with a view through the gates.

Wooden Charm

Head straight down Jalan Raja Alang till it meets Jalan Raja Abdullah. Just across the crossroads is the **Kampung Bahru Mosque**. Built around 1924, it was one of the first concrete structures erected in the quarter. Indeed, the charm of Kampung Bahru lies in the architecture and layout of the houses. Typically made of wood, these elevated houses sport Malay architectural features such as the *anjung* or porch for receiving guests, sloping roofs for ventilation, and sometimes, a brick staircase. Often, prayer mats or religious writing grace the doors, underscoring the intense devotion many Muslims have for their religion.

Houses like these line the stretch of Jalan Raja Alang beyond the mosque, though many have been sacrificed for the construction of modern office block structures. The residents do not normally open their homes to the public, but on the rare occasion, it may be possible to gain privileged entry, depending on the predisposition of the occupants.

The road ends in a row of shophouses and a mini-bazaar that comes alive on Saturday nights during the *Pasar Minggu* (Sunday Market). Here, you can indulge in more local foods.

6. Kuala Lumpur City Centre (KLCC) *(see pull-out map)*

Take that mandatory snapshot of the world's tallest buildings; sniff around the shops; stroll through the park; and finish with a *latte* by the fountain.

Starting point is Suria KLCC, the shopping mall at the base of the Petronas Twin Towers. The LRT runs beneath the KLCC, and the station here links underground to the mall

The tallest buildings in the world don't seem that impressive when you're up close and personal to them, merely a whole lot of steel and concrete. Then you read the statistics: 65,000sq m (78,000sq yds) of stainless steel cladding, 160,000 cubic m (209,300 cubic yds) of concrete, and let us not forget the 77,000sq m (92,100sq yds) of glass.

This is basically a shopping itinerary that can start in the afternoon and end at night with a concert or simply relaxing at one of the many coffeeshops overlooking the lake. It is a particularly suitable itinerary for families. The **Petronas Twin Towers** are quite an amazing sight at night, soaring 452m (1,483ft) into a pitch black sky. Full moon nights are particularly mesmerising, and, if you get your vantage point right, the yellow orb appears suspended on imaginary wires between the softly-lit spires.

Completed in 1997, the Twin Towers are the anchor buildings in the 40-ha (100-acre) Kuala Lumpur City Centre (KLCC), one of the largest real estate developments in the world. Situated in the former Kuala Lumpur race course, KLCC comprises offices – which are housed in the Twin Towers as well as the surrounding Maxis and Esso towers; a shopping mall – Suria KLCC; a beautiful landscaped park; and a luxury hotel, the Mandarin Oriental.

Get a bird's eye-view of all of this halfway up the towers, from the Skybridge, the 58.4m (192ft) double-decked passageway that joins both towers at levels 41 and 42. The viewing hours are from 9–10.30am and 2.30–4pm daily except Sunday. Queue up at the ground-floor information desk of Tower Two.

Picture Time

For camera buffs, good angles of the Twin Towers can be had from Jalan Ampang and Jalan Tun Razak, as well as from across the lake in the park. Designed by internationally renowned US-based architect Cesar Pelli, the buildings feature local influences such as Islamic designs on the floorplate. In fact, the choice of the number of storeys – 88 – translates in Chinese to 'double luck'.

At the base of the towers sits the mall, **Suria KLCC** (tel: 382 2828, open daily 10am–10pm), a spacious classy shopping venue with department stores and over 270 speciality shops. In the basement is a mall

Right: the glittering Petronas Twin Towers

city itineraries

within a mall called **Aseana**, which features Southeast Asian handicrafts and products. Have a meal at any of the numerous international eateries, fast-food outlets and food courts. A treat would be a meal in a restaurant overlooking the park, or in one of the cafés that dominate the esplanade front; great for people-watching.

State-owned petroleum corporation, Petronas, who occupy Tower One of the Twin Towers, has an excellent interactive museum on the oil and gas industry. **Petrosains** (opens daily 10am–4 pm, closed Mon) sits on the top floor of Suria. The mall is also home to a small, but classy art gallery, which is also the country's first museum space art gallery.

Green Acres

Once the day cools down a little, explore the lovely **KLCC Park**. Designed by the late Brazilian landscape artist Roberto Burle Marx, the 50-acre (20-ha) garden is artfully laid out, and is great for children, particularly the playground and wading pool. The trees and shrubs in the park comprise mainly indigenous species. About 40 trees have been kept intact throughout the construction and dates to the time when the area was the Selangor Turf Club.

In the grounds is also a *surau*, Muslim prayer hall, featuring a metallic dome and delicate Islamic calligraphy. A jogging track winds around the lake, in the middle of which are fountains and sculptures.

The lit 'dancing' fountains in front of the Suria Esplanade are a favourite with locals. There are supposed to be 150 variations to their 'movements' if you can be bothered to count. Still, they provide great atmosphere for the sidewalk café patrons till well past midnight.

Two other options for late-nighters. You could catch a movie at one of the 10 cinemas at the top level. Culture vultures might opt for a classical or jazz performance at the **Dewan Filharmonik Petronas**, Malaysia's first dedicated classical concert hall. Situated at the podium level, this is a small theatre, but it boasts excellent acoustics and an interesting programme. It is home to the fledgling but enthusiastic Malaysian Philharmonic Orchestra.

7. BATU CAVES *(see pull-out map)*

A challenging walk up to a limestone cave temple filled with Hindu deities and mythological art.

Starting point is Batu Caves, about half an hour north of the city centre. Take a taxi from town. Alternatively, this attraction features in most outer city tours

This one is sure to awaken your calf muscles. No visit to Kuala Lumpur is complete without a trip to the Batu Caves, 13km (8 miles) north of KL, one of the most sacred Hindu shrines, an intrigue for cave ecologists and geologists, and a popular tourist attraction.

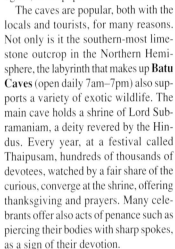

The caves are popular, both with the locals and tourists, for many reasons. Not only is it the southern-most limestone outcrop in the Northern Hemisphere, the labyrinth that makes up **Batu Caves** (open daily 7am–7pm) also supports a variety of exotic wildlife. The main cave holds a shrine of Lord Subramaniam, a deity revered by the Hindus. Every year, at a festival called Thaipusam, hundreds of thousands of devotees, watched by a fair share of the curious, converge at the shrine, offering thanksgiving and prayers. Many celebrants offer also acts of penance such as piercing their bodies with sharp spokes, as a sign of their devotion.

For centuries, the caves were obscured by thick jungle, and known only to locals. In 1878, the caves were discovered by American naturalist William Hornaday. The existence of the caves soon became known to the public and the caves became a popular picnic spot for the colonial masters and their wives. During the Japanese Occupation, Batu Caves served as a hideout for anti-Japanese communist guerilla forces. It was only years later that the local Hindu population, with their predilection for sacred caves, began making pilgrimages here to celebrate the Thaipusam festival.

The Climb

The first thing you will notice as you approach the main gates to the temple is the immense concrete staircase that leads up to the temple caves. There are 272 steps in all, making it quite a climb. Monkeys perch in perfect nonchalance along the staircase, and will quite willingly accept bananas (or for that matter, just about anything else). You can buy fruits and nuts to feed the monkeys at food stalls near the row of shops to the right of the staircase. These monkeys are not tame enough to touch though, and a comfortable distance is well advised.

Once inside the main cave, take care to observe reli-

Left: KLCC Park's playground – a delight for children
Top: Batu Caves **Right:** monkeys will greet you along the way

gious sensitivities by respecting those praying and keeping a distance from the shrines. Climb down the steps and once back on *terra firma*, you may want to visit the **Gallery of Indian Art**, located to the left of the staircase. Set in another cave, it features intricate clay figurines and paintings from Indian mythological tales. True to the art form, the sculptures of Indian deities and scenes from Indian mythology are painted with bright, sometimes verging on the garish, colours.

There are a couple of souvenir shops, but besides the 'I was at Batu Caves' pendants, there is nothing you cannot get in the city. One shop specialises in fresh coconut water served in the nut itself. The others serve mainly Indian food at very reasonable prices. One shop specialises in Indian religious paraphernalia such as oil lamps, camphor holders, incense holders and icons. Depending on your taste, this shop can be a collector's paradise.

If you don't like crowds, avoid visiting at weekends, holidays and Thaipusam, when it's almost impossible to move.

8. AGRICULTURE PARK *(see pull-out map)*

See a nutshell of Malaysian agricultural activities; visit the Tropical Fruit Garden and the nearby lakes. Bring a packed meal and drinks for the day; fishing enthusiasts should also bring their own gear.

Starting point is the park itself, about 40 minutes from the city centre. Take the KTM Komuter train to Subang Parade, and take a taxi from there to the park. Arrange for the taxi to pick you up after you're done. Alternatively, take the Intrakota 338 or Cityliner 222 bus from the Klang Bus Station at Jalan Sultan Mohamad

This tour is definitely for those who enjoy nature. Located some 30km (19 miles) from Kuala Lumpur, the **Taman Pertanian Malaysia** (Malaysia Agriculture Park; tel: 550 6922; open daily 9am–5pm) is a showcase of Malaysian agriculture. Carved from 1,295 ha (3,200 acres) of tropical forest in Bukit Cahaya Seri Alam, Shah Alam, the park features many facets of agriculture, livestock and fisheries in rustic surroundings.

The entrance fee to the park includes the cost of the internal bus shuttle service. The bus stops are strategically placed to enable you to visit the various attractions. Decide where you want to get off, and at your chosen stops, walk around, timing yourself to catch the bus to your next stop. Alternatively, you may want to rent bicycles, which lets you cover more ground. The shady trails make cycling enjoyable but make sure you have lots of water with you to avoid dehydration. From the gate, it is only a short walk to the park administration building where

Left: rambutan fruit trees at the Tropical Fruit Gar

you can collect literature and maps on park facilities. Maps are also clearly displayed at all shuttle bus shelters in the park.

A highlight of the park is the **Tropical Fruit Garden**, which has been planted with exotic species such as durian, mangosteen and rambutan trees. These are fruit that you can buy in markets and supermarkets in town. A lot of local fruit are exported fresh, canned or as juice. However, Malaysian fruit are generally best eaten fresh, though some, like the jackfruit, are a popular treat when deep fried in batter. Most local fruit are seasonal, so if you visit outside of the fruit season, you may have to be satisfied with a canopy of dense boughs and dried branches.

Another interesting feature of the park is the paddy field and rice milling plant, reminiscent of paddy fields that dominate the countrysides of many Asian countries. As with most Asian countries, rice is the staple diet in Malaysia. Most of Malaysia's rice fields are found north of Kuala Lumpur in the Sekinchan area, as well as in the northernmost states of Kedah and Perlis, known as the rice bowl of the country. Like all of Malaysia's agricultural sectors, the rice industry has been modernised; machinery and fertilisers have replaced the buffalo, and new fast-growing and disease-resistant rice strains enable at least two harvests a year.

Climb the hill behind the milling plant and walk through the cocoa estate to the fisheries lake. Here, in pleasant surroundings, you can fish to your heart's content in the company of fellow anglers. However, you have to bring your own gear. Even if you don't plan to fish, visit the boat-shaped fisheries centre, which has interesting exhibits on various facets of the local fishing industry.

There are numerous other attractions: the animal park, aviary, fish cages, spice garden, orchid and flower gardens, temperate garden, mushroom garden, and cultural village, but they are a good hike or ride away and would take up most of the day. Just follow the maps at the bus shelters, or those you might have collected at the administration building.

Above: a model rice field at the Agriculture Park

Shady Options

For hikers, clearly defined trails lead through the forest to isolated destinations. One of these goes to **Sapu Tangan Hill**, which also takes in the Air Kuning and Sungai Baru lakes.

Air Kuning Lake is an angler's retreat in the middle of a tropical forest. However, many locals come here just for the relaxing atmosphere. Pho-

tographers especially will find many opportunities for great outdoor shots. **Sungai Baru Lake** features a 'cage culture' complex where fish varieties like the *tilapia*, river catfish, sultan fish and other exotics, are reared in submerged cages. There is no charge for entering the cage complex area.

The park also has a hydroponics garden and aviary. Within the park, chalet-style accommodation (tel: 550 7048 for reservations) designed to mimic life in a traditional Malay *kampung* is available for larger groups. There are also chalets for four with and without facilities.

There are a number of stalls at the park serving drinks and food. Some of the more isolated stalls only open during weekends and holidays. However, the canteen near the rice fields is usually open.

After this, it is time to head back to the city. If you had negotiated with the taxi driver for a return trip earlier, ask to be driven back to your hotel.

9. SUNWAY LAGOON *(see pull-out map)*

Spend the morning at the Sunway Lagoon theme park; lunch and shop at the Sunway Pyramid Shopping Centre; then take a walk through the Sunway Resort Hotel.

Starting point is Sunway Lagoon in Petaling Jaya, about half-an-hour from the city centre. Take the KTM Komuter train to the Subang Jaya Station and then a taxi to the theme park

This is a fun-filled itinerary for the entire family while theme park lovers will have a splashing good time. **Sunway Lagoon** (tel: 735 8000; open Mon and Wed–Fri 12–7.30pm; weekends and public holidays 10am–7.30pm; open on Tues only during school and public holidays) is Malaysia's best-known and most popular theme park, and part of the Sunway City 'Resort Living within the City' development. Weekends are the busiest days, and December, always the busiest month. Although the park can accommodate up to 70,000 visitors a day, it might be a good idea to avoid the peak periods altogether. The cover charge is high, but there are options to visit individual parks as well as all three.

Fashioned from 324ha (800 acres) of rehabilitated mining and quarry-

Above: landscaped gardens in Agriculture Park
Right: Sunway Pyramid Shopping Centre

ing land, Sunway Lagoon comprises three sections. The original water theme park, the Waterpark (open 4–5pm, 6–7pm) is home to the world's largest surf pool, with huge waves that can rear up to almost 1.5-m (5-ft) high. You can rent tubes, boogie boards, body boards, surf boards for pools, and lockers to store your personal belongings.

A 48-m (160-ft) long escalator links the Waterpark to the Adventure Park. This park features seven rides, and a 428m (1,400ft) pedestrian suspension bridge across the lake. From this vantage point, there are great views of the Waterpark. There is also an indoor games arcade for children.

The third park is the Fort Lagoon Wild Wild West, based on the American Wild West. Spread across 2ha (5 acres), this park features seven rides, including the Buffalo Bill Coaster around the 'Grand Canyon' complete with Red Indian Chief, and the Niagara Falls Flume Ride up a giant rattlesnake and down into a pool.

When you get hungry from all those rides, there are four food outlets in the complex, offering mainly fast food; one dishes out local fare too. Those who just want to have a look at the park can get quite a nice view from the neighbouring **Sunway Pyramid Shopping Centre**. Fronted by a quirky giant lion's head *a la* the sphynx and 'carvings' of ancient Egyptians pushing shopping carts, this mall has a selection of speciality shops as well as the usual department stores. It also has an ice skating rink, a 48-lane bowling centre where the Malaysian national bowling squad practise, and 10 cineplexes. For food, there is a choice of over 40 outlets.

Another quirky attraction in the area is the **Sunway Lagoon Resort Hotel** (tel: 03-582 8000, www.jaring.my/hotel/sunmain.htm), a five-star property styled after the famous Sun City in South Africa. The hotel has nice accommodations and excellent restaurants, including the funky Avanti, an American-Italian restaurant.

10. CHOW KIT *(see map below)*

Shopping at The Mall and an early dinner at Medan Hang Tuah; a walk down Chow Kit; and an open-air bazaar.

Starting point is The Mall, close to the Putra World Trade Centre, and within walking distance to the Putra KTM Komuter Station

Mention **Chow Kit** to any KL-ite and watch the sly grins spreading over their faces. There is a good reason for it, Chow Kit was once the most notorious neighbourhood in the city. Today, urban renewal has sanitised much of what was once KL's sleaze centre. But old impressions die hard. Besides, such things are not easily suppressed. In the backlanes and dark alleys of a Chow Kit evening, transvestites still ply their trade and call girls stare from behind masks of cheap make-up.

Chow Kit is home to a chic shopping plaza, The Mall, at the end of **Jalan Putra**. Begin your walk from here. Early evening is a good time to explore this area. Opposite The Mall is the sprawling **Putra World Trade Centre** (PWTC) where consumer and trade exhibitions are held. Inside this complex are the headquarters of UMNO, the ruling party, a concert venue, and the Tourism Malaysia headquarters. Tourist information is available at its office on the ground floor.

On the other side of Jalan Putra from the PWTC is **Perhentian Putra**, the bus station for express coaches to and from the east coast of the peninsula. Adjacent to the PWTC is the **Pan Pacific Hotel Kuala Lumpur**, where you can sample local hawker fare in its air-conditioned brasserie, Selera Restaurant, while observing the bustle along Jalan Putra. Alternatively, hit The Mall.

The Mall houses a host of shops, including the Aktif Lifestyle department store, which has a decent range of clothing. Taking up almost half of the fourth floor is a food court called **Medan Hang Tuah**. Modelled on Kuala Lumpur

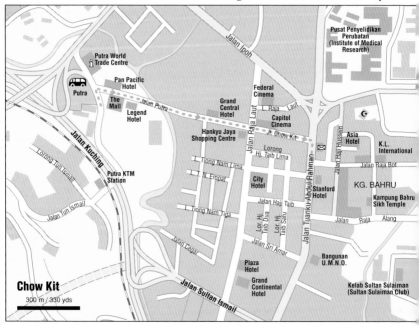

Chow Kit
300 m / 330 yds

city itineraries

in the 1930s, doorways, street lights and building facades of the period have been painstakingly recreated. The food court offers an immense variety of Malay and Chinese food. Have an early dinner here.

After checking out The Mall, head down Jalan Putra towards **Jalan Chow Kit**, about a 15-minute walk, or a short taxi ride away. Adjoining The Mall is the **Legend Hotel**, which has an excellent if expensive fine dining Chinese restaurant, the Museum, and the Monkey Bar, where you occasionally get good bands. Continue past the crossroads to **Jalan Tuanku Abdul Rahman**. The Chow Kit Bus Stand here is where you can get buses to the trendy and upmarket suburb of Bangsar for a completely different cosmopolitan experience. Buses from here also go to Jalan Genting Kelang, and thence to the National Zoo and Aquarium. This point marks the beginning of the Chow Kit shopping zone, a bazaar so elaborate that only major landmarks are given.

Start on the side of the road you are now on and walk in the direction of the traffic. All the stores lining the street have cheap goods. The sidewalk, in the meantime, becomes noticeably crowded, as vendors open up stalls that sell what seems like everything under the sun. It gets even better on the opposite stretch. Continue walking down the road and use the crossing to get to the other side. The bazaar here occupies (though 'congests' is a better word) not only the sidewalks of Jalan Tuanku Abdul Rahman, but the side streets as well. This is the place for one of the most colourful and lively night markets. The authorities have long since given up on ensuring vehicular traffic flow, and pedestrians have taken over. Buses fly down this road with horns blaring; don't get in their path!

The range of goods is extensive, but as in Chinatown, do not be deceived by fake designer labels and brands. Prices are inflated so don't be shy of bargaining; it is not unusual to get discounts of at least 20 percent. When you get peckish, there are lots of street food for sale. Try the Malay favourites of *rending* beef curry, the less spicy-hot chicken *kurma*, or the ubiquitous Malay MacDonald's knock-off, Ramli Burger.

Above: a cosmetics shop at The Mall
Right: an ethnic crafts shop

11. JALAN TUANKU ABDUL RAHMAN *(see map below)*

Lunch at the Coliseum Café; wander down Jalan Tuanku Abdul Rahman and explore the Masjid India area; visit Little India and enjoy a North Indian dinner.

Starting point is the Coliseum Café and Hotel, about five minutes' walk from the Bandaraya LRT Station and the Bank Negara KTM Komuter Station

Built in 1928, the **Coliseum Café and Hotel** located next to the Coliseum Cinema on Jalan Tuanku Abdul Rahman has definitely seen better days. Its original decor, mismatched furniture and fittings disguise a once popular drinking hole for prosperous colonial planters, tin miners and traders. It still serves good, hearty meals served by sullen-faced Hainanese Chinese waiters, traditionally chefs for the colonials, and makes for an interesting (and reasonably-priced) meal. The sizzling steaks are recommended if you start your tour with lunch here. A relic of early Kuala Lumpur, the café's facade has been maintained and provides sharp contrast to nearby fast-food outlets. Notice how the café blends the antiquity of the city with 20th-century slickness. Upstairs are modest guest rooms at reasonable rates.

After lunch, join the crowds on the pavements of **Jalan Tuanku Abdul Rahman**, the city's longest shopping street and named after the first king of independent Malaysia. To the locals, however, this area is popularly known as Batu Road. Merchandise ranging from textiles and carpets to shoes and leather goods are hawked by both shop and sidewalk vendors. There are also many *kedai makan* or 'eating shops', some of whose food should definitely be sampled.

From the Coliseum Café, head left. One of the first shops is **Minerva Bookstore**, specialising in Islamic literature. English titles are also available. Minerva's has another store on the opposite side of the road. Further on, the **Central Shoe Store** has one of largest range of footwear in the city. Other stores sell a variety of goods from sporting gear to textiles. **Sogo Department Store** on your left is a gigantic Japanese outlet with a supermarket, bookshop, restaurants, and a slew of luxury and bargain goods. Its periodic sales are good value.

Age-old Stores

You are now at the junction of Jalan Tuanku Abdul Rahman and Jalan Dang Wangi. Cross the street and backtrack along the opposite side. Shoppers will experience a bizarre feeling of tranquillity on this road, despite the bustling atmosphere. With its mix of new

Top right: fabrics of all colours and de
Right: Jalan Tuanku Abdul Rahman

shopping malls and established older stores, this strip offers an eclectic blend of consumer options. The **Peiping Lace** and the **China Arts Co** at No 217 and 223 are two Chinese-run stores selling quality antiques that are worth a browse.

One of the country's oldest department stores, **Globe Silk Store**, located further down, offers some of the cheapest clothing buys in the city. There are five floors of clothing including batik shirts and the Malay *baju kurung* womenswear, textiles, cosmetics and carpets in the Globe, while the top floor has a very nice caféteria. You may want to take a break with a cold drink and curry puff (pastry stuffed with curried vegetables and meat) here.

Further down the street are two more well-established names, the **P Lal Store** and **Chotirmall Store**. There are several textile stores along the way where fabrics and garments from all over Asia are sold. Although prices are generally fixed in the larger department stores, it is possible to bargain at the smaller shops.

Yet further down the road more restaurants and textile stores are located within the 'five-foot-way', the local term for a shaded footpath. There are a few shops selling costume jewellery, hair bands and other accessories. The prices vary according to the quality, but be prepared to bargain.

On Saturday evenings, the street is turned into a pedestrian mall and a night market sprouts up along the entire stretch. Like all night markets in Malaysia, the prices are low and the variety is staggering. Vendors sell everything, from fresh meat and vegetables to clothes and household items. Try not to miss this night bazaar – the atmosphere alone is worth experiencing.

Continuing down the street, you will first meet the junction with Jalan Melayu, then the major intersection with Jalan Tun Perak and the overhead LRT track. Turn left into Jalan Tun Perak. The Moorish structure across the road was built during the colonial days and now accommodates courthouses.

As you walk down Jalan Tun Perak, you will pass on the left the Bank

of Commerce building before coming to Jalan Melayu and the Masjid Jamek LRT Station (opposite its namesake, the Jame Mosque). Turn into Jalan Melayu. Across the road, the Klang River is undergoing a major clean-up.

On your left are a row of shops that specialise in Indian *sarees* and fabrics. Among them are restaurants that dish up Indian breads and curries. This is an excellent opportunity to try a cold yoghurt-based drink called *lassi*. Opt for the sweetened or fruit-based version. There is a range of Indian desserts on sale, including a diabetes-inducing orange-coloured sweet called *jelabi*, and *gulab jamun*, a round milk fritter soaked in syrup.

Sarees and Incense

Cross the road into **Jalan Masjid India**, an area of marked Indian-Muslim accent. Every available space on Jalan Masjid India, which runs parallel to Jalan Tuanku Abdul Rahman, is taken up by shops, restaurants and a colourful blend of pavement stalls. Among them are artists, and the ubiquitous pavement medicine seller whose concoctions can allegedly cure any ailment from snake bites to sexual maladies. For pure theatrical appeal, it is hard to beat the style of these street peddlers; a sure crowd-puller with their fast-paced narration of unbelievable medicinal wonders. Despite language barriers, it's possible to get a general idea of what they're touting.

Jalan Masjid India begins, ironically, with a cluster of Malay shops (Wisma Yakin) on your right. The shops sell clothes and food as well as *jamu*, a traditional cure-all medicine made from grounded herbs. Many Malays swear by this stuff, which reportedly also works wonders for the libido. On the left is **Masjid India**, an Indian-Muslim mosque after which the street is named. Although it is only open to Muslim worshippers, do stop to appreciate its typically Indian-Muslim architecture. There are also good camera opportunities, but be very discreet and respect the worshippers' right to decline being photographed.

Jalan Masjid India proper is best known for its speciality shops dealing in Indian textiles, Indian ethnic music tapes, ethnic handmade jewellery,

Above: pavement medicine men along Jalan Masjid India offer traditional massage

city itineraries

religious icons, brassware and other exotica. As you stroll down the road, buy a cooling drink of *mata kuching* (longan fruit tea) or coconut juice from one of the many drink vendors. The road branches into a fork in front of the Selangor Mansion; the narrower street on the right is **Medan Bunus**. The broad divider explodes in a blaze of colour with buckets of freshly-cut blooms and religious garlands displayed on wire enclosures. The flower-sellers here will thread the blossoms into anything you want, from simple hair adornments to lavish bridal car arrangements.

Back onto Masjid India, the shops continue down the street. On your left is **Car and Company**, one of the country's oldest and best known sporting goods stores. Nearby are the budget accommodation-styled Chamtan, Palace and Empire hotels. They are popular with foreign backpackers, not surprising given their colourful ambience, central location and access to cheap, good food. At the end of the street are more shops, including money changers, a pharmacy and clothing stores. Indian cutlery stores along this row specialise in Indian stainless steel cutlery.

Masjid India terminates when you see a shopping mall called **Semua House**. There are a few shops here that sell costume jewellery, clothes, video cassettes and other merchandise. Exit left from Semua House, walk past City One Plaza, turn right at the end of the street and walk through the carpark. From here, be careful not to miss the tiny, almost kitschy, Hindu temple en route. Leave the temple, go left and return to Jalan Masjid India. Retrace your steps back to Jalan Tun Perak and the Masjid Jamek LRT Station. Turn left and walk towards the traffic lights at Lebuh Ampang.

Historic Street

On the left, just before the traffic lights, is the Masjid Jamek LRT Station, with a monstrous MacDonald's beside it. Turn left into Lebuh Ampang and continue into Little India. The area still has a distinctly Indian feel; try a bag of mixed spicy Indian munchies. Several shops deal in Indian-style filigree 22-karat gold. Indian jewellery is traditionally chunkier and more ornate than Western gold jewellery. There are also some *kittingai* behind metallic concertina doors, Indian *chettiar* money-lending outlets that once ruled the street and indeed, funded many of the economic activities of locals before World War II.

Continue to the end of the street and turn right into Jalan Gereja, past St John's Cathedral and Jalan Bukit Nanas. At the junction of Jalan Raja Chulan is the restored neo-classical **Muzium Telekom** (tel: 201 9966; open 9.30am–5pm, closed Monday), which charts Malaysia's telecommunications history and features hi-tech displays. The 1928 building used to house a pre-war manual telephone exchange.

Return to your hotel, freshen up for dinner and catch a taxi to **Bangles** (tel: 298 6770) restaurant on 60A Jalan Tuanku Abdul Rahman. This restaurant serves good North Indian dishes such as *tandoori* and *kebabs*, accompanied by slabs of hot oven-baked bread called *naan*. Wash the meal down with spicy Indian *masala* tea.

Right: a Muslim faithful in traditional garb

12. KLANG VALLEY *(see pull-out map)*

A trip to the richest and fastest-growing area in Malaysia, followed by a seafood dinner in Port Klang.

Starting point is the predominantly Indian suburb of Brickfields, 15 minutes' walk from the Kuala Lumpur Railway Station. Alternatively, catch a taxi there

This bus or train tour takes you down the **Klang Valley**, the most dynamic, wealthiest and industrialised region in the country. The route is roughly parallel to the Klang River. Just 130 years ago, a group of miners led a prospecting expedition up the same river in search of tin and ended up founding Malaysia's capital city, Kuala Lumpur. The Klang Valley then was totally inhospitable with impenetrable jungle and swamp. Much of this has disappeared with urbanisation.

Kuala Lumpur's first link with the outside world was via a railway line built by Sir Frank Swettenham in 1886. Today, sleek, electric commuter trains service the route from Port Klang to Rawang in the north. Regular services leave Kuala Lumpur Railway Station, Platform 2A, for Pelabuhan Klang (Port Klang) and it is preferable to catch the train for at least one leg of this trip.

Start with breakfast, or an early lunch of *yong tau foo* (stuffed *tofu* and vegetables) at the stall along **Jalan Thambapillay** at the T-junction with Jalan Tun Sambanthan in Brickfields. For drinks, a nearby stall sells sugar cane juice and coconut water.

After lunch, take a taxi to the **Klang Bus Station**. The express bus services to Klang are easily located and are operated by the Klang Banting Express Line. Comfortable, air-conditioned buses leave every half hour or so. Just board a bus and wait for the conductor to approach you for the fare.

The first area the bus passes is the massive railroad yard at Brickfields, near where you ate earlier. A century ago, the kilns of Brickfields supplied all the requirements of a rapidly growing town. The name still sticks despite the fact that the kilns were relocated long ago. A central transport terminal is being built here.

The bus passes through **Jalan Bangsar**, then swings onto the eight-lane Federal Highway, the main road link to Klang. Just after entering the highway, you pass under an archway that signals the division between the restless urban sprawl of Kuala Lumpur and its less frenzied satellite town, **Petaling Jaya**.

Suburbia

Petaling Jaya, sensibly abbreviated to PJ, was developed originally as a low-cost housing scheme in the late 1950s. It has since blossomed into a middle-class area of over 500,000 inhabitants who incidentally have the highest rate

Left: local girls in school uniform

of personal car ownership in Southeast Asia. After PJ, the bus goes past **Sungai Way**, a suburb of PJ (when a satellite town begins to have its own suburb, you know it has arrived) where most of the electronics factories are located. PJ merges into another middle-class suburb, **Subang Jaya**.

The bus then enters **Shah Alam**, the capital of the state of Selangor, which was hewn in the 1970s out of rubber plantations, and is one of the country's best planned cities with broad boulevards and huge roundabouts. The highway traverses the town, dividing it into two distinct sections: on the left its industrial face, already larger than that of PJ and still growing; and on the right its residential enclave.

Within the High Technology Park on the left, though not visible from the bus, is the Perusahaan Otomobil Nasional (Proton) factory, Malaysia's first national car manufacturer, whose products dominate the roads. Further, on the right is the towering spire and distinctive powder-blue dome of the **Masjid Sultan Salahuddin Abdul Aziz Shah** (Blue Mosque), the grand Selangor state mosque. Next to the mosque, the skyline is dominated by the office towers of downtown Shah Alam.

While there is little semblance of a green belt between Shah Alam and Klang, the distinction between the two towns is marked. Klang is old, in fact, older than Kuala Lumpur. The streets meander between pre-World War II shops, houses and overgrown rain trees. About 10km (6 miles) to the west is **Pelabuhan Klang** (Port Klang), Malaysia's biggest and busiest port, but the town after which it is named seems totally unaffected by the massive efforts to modernise and upgrade it.

Those who arrive in Klang by bus will find only one word for it: bedlam, located as it is in that part of the town centre where most of the larger supermarkets and department stores operate. As you exit the bus depot you will notice a taxi stand in front of the largest department store. The train station is not well serviced by taxis, but wait patiently. There are no tour bus facilities operational in Klang, so you would have to hire a taxi to tour the city. The rate varies according to the length of time you hire the taxi

Above: the Blue Mosque at sunset

for, but generally it is about RM15 per hour. Agree upon the rate before boarding the taxi.

The one-time capital of Selangor, Klang is completely overshadowed economically by Shah Alam. However, while Shah Alam has been planned and efficienctly built, Klang is far more colourful and exuberant. In addition, its long and proud history has left its mark on the town.

For much of its past, the Bugis, a maritime people from the Celebes Islands (now Indonesia's Sulawesi), played a dominant role in Klang's palace politics. In fact, Klang was one of the three capitals of the state, the other two being Kuala Langat and Kuala Selangor. As the warlords in each capital set out to establish their hegemony, conflict was inevitable. The 1867 Selangor Civil War was one of the most significant milestones in Klang's history. In the end, it established Klang's dominance as the state capital and, consequently, its development as a major metropolis.

Pre-war Structures

Tell the taxi driver to take you around the town centre. Unlike Kuala Lumpur, Klang never went through a rash of urbanisation in which lovely old homes and shophouses were torn down and replaced with glass-and-steel cuboids. Much of Klang town still retains a lot of its old character; many buildings have been around since World War II.

Start your tour by telling the taxi driver to take you to the **Kota Raja Mahadi** on Jalan Kota. It is a fort built by one of the protagonists in the 1867 Civil War. Across the town, along Jalan Tepi Sungai, is **Gedung Raja Abdullah**. It was built in 1856 by Raja Mahadi's opponent, Raja Abdullah, who played a key role in the founding of Kuala Lumpur through the prospecting of tin. The warehouse, which typifies traditional Malay architecture, has been converted into the **Tin Museum** (open daily 9am–4pm), bringing back Klang's exciting past to life.

On Jalan Timur is the venerable **Sultan Sulaiman Mosque**, built by the British in the 19th century and given to Sultan Sulaiman. It has an interesting blend of British Imperial, Moorish and Arabic architectural styles. A British architect designed the mosque.

Another building that features a similar blend of architectural styles is the **Istana Alam Shah**, the palace of the Sultan of Selangor, located on Jalan Istana. The Sultan no longer resides here but in Shah Alam. However, the palace is still maintained for official functions. It is not open to the public, but is visible some 100m (330ft) to the left (as you face the main gate) from where you can enjoy a panoramic view of the palace and its grounds. Unfortunately, parking is difficult.

The above tour sequence takes you from one side of Klang town to the other. After you have finished touring the town, it should be close to late evening. Round off the day with a sumptuous seafood meal at Port Klang. Once known as Port Swettenham, it is the major seaport for Kuala Lumpur and the Klang Valley.

Above: crest at Sultan Sulaiman Mosque
Right: Sultan Sulaiman Mosque is a blend of different architectural styles

2. GENTING HIGHLANDS *(see pull-out map)*

Take a journey to the cool hills and enjoy the exhilaration of a highland theme park and casino.

To starting point: Bus or taxi from Puduraya Bus and Taxi Station

Genting Highlands – perched on top of the Titiwangsa mountain range that runs down the centre of the peninsula – is one of Kuala Lumpur's most popular recreation destinations. It boasts a family-oriented theme park, the country's largest theatre restaurant and its only legal casino. With other attractions like an 18-hole golf course, cable cars, restaurants, amusement parks and a boating lake, and given the fact that Genting Highlands is only 48km (30 miles) from Kuala Lumpur, it is little surprise that the retreat gets very crowded at weekends and school holidays. Located some 2,000m (6,500ft) above sea level, the midday temperature at Genting Highlands ranges from a cool 16–23°C (60–72°F), a respite from the city heat.

There are several ways of getting to Genting Highlands. The cheapest is by air-conditioned buses from the Puduraya Bus Station. Express buses run every half hour between 7.30am and 7pm (tel: 232 6863). The fare is inclusive of the 13-minute cable car ride from the base of the hill to the **Genting Highlands Resort** (tel: 03-262 3555) at the peak. The resort comprises five hotels and apartments, all of which are inter-linked. The cable car service operates 24 hours a day. If you're booked into the **Awana Golf and Country Resort** (tel: 03-261 9888) midway up, you take a shuttle from the base. Taxis also operate from Puduraya and deliver you directly to your hotel. Besides the golf course, Awana has splendid scenery, jungle treks and waterfalls. A shut-

tle links the Awana to the main Gentings Highland Resort.

Once at the resort, clear directional signs make it easy to find your way around. If visiting the casino, make sure that you are appropriately dressed. Men are required to wear ties with long-sleeved shirts or a jacket without tie. Alternatively, the traditional Malaysian *batik* shirt is acceptable – these can be rented at the entrance. The casino strictly forbids Muslims from entering, in accordance with the Islamic prohibition against gambling.

Genting's amusement park will keep non-gamblers busy. The outdoor theme park, set around an artificial lake, has rollercoasters, boat rides, and a monorail. The indoor theme park, with stunning virtual reality displays, is the largest video/virtual reality arcade in Malaysia. There are also two theatres which feature international magic performances or cabaret dinner shows. Note: there are no cheap eateries and the only food outlets, both Western and local, are hotel restaurants and coffee shops.

Left: Istana Bandar in Jugra
Above: Genting Highlands theme park

3. PULAU KETAM *(see pull-out map)*

Relax in a picturesque fishing village and feast on some of Malaysia's wonderful seafood.

To starting point: KTM Komuter to Pelabuhan Klang, then a taxi to the public jetty at Port Klang, and finally the ferry to the island

A day trip with a difference, **Pulau Ketam** (Crab Island) is 1½ hours away by boat from **Port Klang**.

Pulau Ketam is reputed to be the last Chinese fishing village in the state of Selangor. The lights and salaries of big city life in Kuala Lumpur, so close by, have enticed many a youngster away from the traditional occupations of their forefathers.

The jetty to the island at Port Klang is a good place to take interesting photos of fresh fish that is constantly unloaded from boats. Ferry services to the island start at 7am and operate every hour. The last ferry leaves the island at 6pm. There is also the option of hiring one of the fast boats, which cuts the journey right down; be sure to negotiate the price before you step on board.

When the island's intrepid pioneers discovered it about a century ago, Pulau Ketam was nothing more than a mangrove mudpile that almost disappeared during high tide. Instead of looking for greener pastures, they stayed put, building their houses on stilts. Today, a whole township, complete with sidewalks, groceries, power station, telephone exchange and bars, all on stilts, has developed on the island.

Everything on the island revolves around fishing: catching it, transporting it to the mainland, or servicing the industry. Although it is illegal for fishing vessels to carry passengers, it has not stopped the fishermen of Pulau Ketam from openly soliciting anglers, especially in the weekends.

Above: stilt houses line Pulau Ketam's banks
Left: away from the mayhem of city life

The town's restaurants serve some of the finest seafood around. Try the **Nam Hong** or **Kim Hor** restaurants, both renowned for the island speciality, ie steamed *sembilang* or catfish. Visitors from as far away as Singapore think nothing of making their way to Pulau Ketam just for the seafood.

As Teochew and Cantonese people mainly live on the island, the cooking style is Chinese. The seafood can be cooked in various ways but it is usually not *halal* (taboo) for Muslims, so ask first.

Local Night Treats

If you want to spend the night, the only billeting of any quality on Pulau Ketam is the **Ketam Island Village Lodge**. Located conveniently at the jetty, the lodge offers basic but clean and comfortable air-conditioned accommodation at very reasonable rates.

If you are staying overnight, there are a couple of karaoke lounges and nightclubs on the island. They are all within the immediate vicinity of the Ketam Island Village Lodge. You should be warned that the nightclub acts are known to get raunchy at times, but that has never stopped anyone from having a good time.

The journey to the island could be tedious as the boat travels through the rather monotonous landscape of mangrove swamps. Cleanliness is also not the islanders' strong point. However, as Pulau Ketam was built to serve the needs of the local community, it is the perfect place to soak in the atmosphere of a lively fishing village. Except for a short stroll around the fishing village and a meal at the seafood restaurants, there are no other tourist attractions. Two or three hours here would be more than sufficient. It is also possible to visit nearby fish farms from here, so ask around.

4. FOREST RESEARCH INSTITUTE OF MALAYSIA (FRIM)
(see pull-out map)

Discover a sprawling tropical rainforest located just on the edge of the city.

To starting point: take a taxi from town; the closest KTM Komuter Station is at Kepong, but it could be difficult to get taxis from there

The oldest jungles in the world are the tropical rainforests of Southeast Asia and South America. Looking at Kuala Lumpur today though, it is difficult to believe that the city was once covered in dense tropical rainforest. Those who wish to visit an authentic rainforest without travelling too far out of the city need not despair. Tucked away in the hills northwest of Kuala Lumpur is one of the world's oldest forest research centres. Covering some 600ha (1,480 acres), the **Forest Research Institute of Malaysia** (FRIM) is a showcase for the incredible variety of flora and fauna found within a tropical lowland forest.

Opened in 1926, FRIM has gained increasing popularity among KL-ites and visitors as a peaceful retreat from city living. Located some 16km (10 miles)

Right: one of Malaysia's myriad butterflies rests on a hibiscus

from the city, it is most easily reached by taxi. There are no bus services to FRIM, so arrange with your taxi driver to pick you from the institute later. If you're driving, you will have to pay a nominal entry charge for your car.

Once there, finding your way around the well-signposted park is easy. You may wish to pick up maps of the grounds from the public relations office. The nature trails and jungle tracks are shown on these maps, with explanations of the vegetation you can expect to see.

Since this park is dedicated to environmental science research, every attempt has been made to conserve the forest ecosystem. You would notice on your way in that all the signs, buildings and houses are environmentally-friendly and the structures appear to blend with the surroundings. Traditional wooden houses constructed without the use of nails can also be visited. There is also a museum (open daily 9am–5pm) and a nursery.

One of the most significant features of any tropical forest is its multi-canopied structure, each canopy being a sub-ecosystem in its own right. Unfortunately, this feature is among the first to disappear with tourist development. In FRIM, the authorities have taken pains to preserve the multi-tiered canopies of the forest.

Mini Showcases

After picking up literature at the public relations office, wander through the various arboretums. There are six of these, showcasing indigenous fruit trees, conifers, monocotyledenous trees, dipterocarps and non-dipterocarps. Dipterocarps are the largest tree family in Malaysia, covering almost three-quarters of the natural forested areas. The trees in the various arboretums are clearly labelled so that visitors can identify what they see.

Of FRIM's many nature trails, the Keruing nature trail is the shortest, beginning behind the library and ending at the fishpond. The jungle tracks are longer and reach deeper into the forest. Early morning and late evening are when the forest is noisiest. A cicada chorus can be accompanied by the sounds of crickets and the numerous calls of birds, which you might just hear if you move quietly and in small enough numbers through the forest.

There is only one caféteria in the park, so if you're planning a hike up to the waterfall, you may want to buy food and drinks from the canteen next to the gymnasium. Alternatively, bring a packed lunch and picnic in the forest. The park organises day trips for groups of over 40 people, but such excursions have to be pre-booked. If you plan to camp overnight, obtain permission from the park authorities first.

The best time to visit the tropical forest park is in the early morning or late evening when the air is freshest and walking in the shady rainforest is usually relatively cool. Remember to drink lots of water.

5. KUALA SELANGOR *(see pull-out map)*

Explore a ruined fortress, a lighthouse and a mausoleum. Go bird-watching in a nature park, enjoy a seafood meal and see the river light up with fireflies.

To starting point: Catch the very slow local bus from the Puduraya Bus & Taxi Station, or for the better alternative, hire a taxi for the day from there; the journey takes 1½ hours by taxi

Standing at the estuary of the Selangor River, **Kuala Selangor** was once the capital to the Sultanate of Selangor. Back then, the river was a vital means of communication to the otherwise impenetrable interior. The Selangor River was also the key to political and economic power: those who controlled communications along the river also controlled the hinterland. The state of Selangor, in this respect, had three great river systems – the Langat, Klang and Selangor – and the respective nobilities that controlled these rivers constantly bickered for dominance. Ultimately, the group controlling the Klang became pre-eminent. Today, the Klang Valley is the nation's fastest growing urban area, while both Kuala Langat and Kuala Selangor have slipped into obscurity.

What greatness the town of Kuala Selangor once knew remains in the form of ruined fortresses, lighthouses and a mausoleum. This excursion is best done in the afternoon if you want to see the fireflies in the evening. You need at least six hours. Alternatively, go on an organised tour. If you plan to spend the night, the **Kuala Selangor Resthouse** (tel: 03-889 1357) offers reasonable rates and simple meals.

Two forts were built to defend the town. The larger and the only one open to the public is **Kota**

Left: a canopy of trees at FRIM **Above:** a house built without nails **Right:** the Altingsburg Lighthouse

Melawati (formerly Fort Altings-burg), which stands on Bukit Mela-wati. It is 100m (330ft) diagonally opposite the resthouse, although vegetation obscures the view of the fort from the resthouse.

From the fort, you can easily walk to other interesting places nearby, including the **Altingsburg Lighthouse**, which is still functional, and the **Royal Mausoleum**, which enshrines the remains of Selangor's ancient Bugis kings. Either walk or drive to **Kuala Selangor Nature Park** (tel: 03-889 2294) at the base of the hill away from the town. A nominal entry fee helps maintain the park which is operated by the Malaysian Nature Society. Simple chalet accommodation and facilities are available for overnight, something which avid birdwatchers would appreciate in order to catch the prolific birdlife feeding at the park at dawn.

Migratory waterbirds are the main attractions here but there are monkeys and otters as well. There are stands of mangrove and secondary forest and a brackish lake system with boardwalks to provide access to the wildlife. A shop rents binoculars and sells souvenirs.

Head back to Kuala Selangor town, which has a few good seafood restaurants. Enjoy an early evening meal and then travel to **Kampung Kuantan**, 9km (5½ miles) south of Kuala Selangor. After 8pm, boats take visitors on a 40-minute ride on the river through trees lined with tiny luminescent fireflies. The millions of tiny male beetles flashing synchronously in the dark is an amazing sight indeed. But be sure to avoid rainy nights, as there would then be fewer fireflies to behold.

6. FRASER'S HILL *(see pull-out map)*

Enjoy highland weather and breathtaking views from this hill resort; explore jungle trails and tee off at the picturesque golf course.

To starting point: Rent a car or catch a taxi for this tour. Alternatively, take a one-hour bus journey from Kuala Lumpur city centre to Kuala Kubu Baharu (100km/60 miles), and another 1½ hours' bus trip up a narrow and winding road (8km/5 miles) to the top. Book accommodation ahead as this is an overnight trip

The road from Kuala Kubu Baharu to **Fraser's Hill** (Bukit Fraser) in Selangor is so narrow that a one-way traffic system is in place between 7am and 7pm; odd hours for going up, even for coming down. It was along this winding road that British High Commissioner Sir Henry Gurney was ambushed and killed by communist guerillas in 1951. If you arrive at the gate too early, you could have tea at the Gap Resthouse, or else drive down to a small but scenic waterfall along the main road that leads to the town of Raub.

Fraser's Hill is named after Louis James Fraser, an elusive English ad-

Above: chalets at Kuala Selangor Nature Park

venturer, who had long disappeared when the hill station was built in 1910. He apparently ran a notorious gambling and opium den here for local miners and planters, as well as a mule train.

An English Air

The 1,500-m (5,000-ft) high resort is scattered over seven hills on which sit a series of English greystone bungalows, surrounded by neat English gardens blooming with roses and hollyhocks. The tiny town centre around the clock tower has some rather disastrous newer additions, and there are also high-rise hotels which fail to blend with the landscape.

A better bet is to go with the economical if run-down bungalows, now state-run. The prettiest and most expensive accommodation is **The Smokehouse Hotel** (tel: 09-362 2226), a replica of the original Smokehouse Hotel in Cameron Highlands, where you can enjoy Devonshire tea or apple pie in the lovely garden. The road to the hotel leads on to Jeriau Waterfall, once a pretty picnic spot, but now permanently silted, the result of short-sighted resort development years ago.

Because of its proximity to Kuala Lumpur, Fraser's is crowded at weekends, but there are enough walks and trails to take you away from the madding crowd. The ring road around the 9-hole golf course makes a pleasant two-hour walk, and brings you past the old bungalows and newer resorts. The picturesque golf course is very old. It was carved out of an old tin mine, and is one of the few public courses in the country.

There are also eight jungle trails of varying lengths, all named after pioneers who built up the resort. The trails are well-marked and easy to follow. The newest is the steep 6-km (4-mile) **Pine Hill Trail** which leads to breathtaking views. The trails run through hilly dipterocarp forests which boasts some of the richest birdlife in the peninsula, hence the high chance of bumping into groups standing rock-still and peering intently through binoculars. There are an estimated 270 local and migratory species in the forest.

If you have your own transport, there are a number of good drives around the area, such as the second loop that goes past the holiday bungalows of multinational corporations.

Right: tee off in Fraser's Hill

Leisure Activities

shopping

SHOPPING

Kuala Lumpur is fast catching up with Singapore, Hong Kong and Bangkok as a shopper's paradise. It also offers some marvellous opportunities for craft collectors and bargain hunters. Worthwhile finds range from antiques and imported spices to religious icons and metalware. Although the law requires retail outlets to affix price tags for all goods sold, bargaining is still an integral part of the Malaysian shopping experience, so be prepared to haggle; the only exception would be in department stores and boutiques.

Traditional Fabrics

One would have thought that gold fabric was a creation of Grecian fables. In Malaysia, it is grounded in reality, and called *songket*. Handed down from the courts of Kelantan in the Peninsula's east coast, and Pattani in Thailand, this cloth is a display of dramatic handwoven tradition featuring intricate tapestry inlaid with gold and metallic threads.

Women in some parts of the Peninsula's east coast still use the traditional two-paddle floor looms to painstakingly interlace threads, with the best pieces coming from Kelantan. *Songket* comes in a multitude of colours that offset the complex tapestry designs, its richness making it more suitable for formal and ceremonial attire. *Songket* material can also be turned into stunning jackets, beautiful evening wear and attractive handbags and shoes.

Batik, the less glamourous cousin of *songket*, has more appeal because of its versatility, durability and price. In fact, *batik* techniques have become so popular, they have become an art form. Also originally from the east coast, *batik* is now printed by factories all over the country, which produces fabrics ranging from cotton and voile to silk and satin. *Batik* is often turned into clothes, accessories, household and decorative items.

Silvercraft and Pewterware

Kelantan silvercraft is one of the most successful cottage industries in Malaysia. It is a craft requiring a great amount of skill, whether in filigree work, where ornamental wire is shaped into delicate tracery, or repousses, where sheet silver is hammered into patterned relief. Kelantan silver is turned into a variety of items, from brooches and costume jewellery to serving dishes and tableware.

Kuala Lumpur's own local handicraft, Royal Selangor pewterware, enjoys a worldwide reputation for its stylish and attractive handmade designs. Pewter is an alloy of tin mixed with a little copper and antimony and was introduced to Malaysia from China in the 18th century. The hardness of the metal gives it durability, and its silvery finish does not tarnish. Using traditional methods of casting and soldering, hundreds of items ranging from tableware, candelabra and ornamental pieces to lapel pins, figurines and pendants are crafted.

Kites and Tops

The traditional *wau* and *gasing* (kites and tops), for which the Peninsula's east coast is best known, enjoy both local and international popularity. Both are traditional sports, with kite flying dating back to the 1500s.

The *wau* comes in all shapes and sizes. The most popular and the largest is the *wau bulan* or moon kite, measuring 3½m (11½ft) from head to tail and capable of soaring to great heights. Its wooden frame is covered with stiff parchment decorated with designs cut from coloured paper and adorned with colourful streamers. Smaller versions are made as decorative items. Malaysia

Left: Star Hill Centre
Right: *songket* – fabric inlaid with gold threads

Airlines, the national airline, features a stylised *wau* in its logo.

Top spinning is no child's play either, not when the traditional Malay top is about the size of a dinner plate and weighs as much as 5½kg (12lbs). The tops are usually disc shaped, and are carefully balanced for spinning power. A good top in the hands of a skilful player can spin for up to two hours.

Bamboo Products & Beadwork

Cane and wicker are used for furniture and household items. *Mengkuang* (pandanus) leaves are woven into mats, baskets, hats and decorative items, and split bamboo strips are shaped into trays, baskets, food covers and household items.

In Sarawak, *nipah* palm reeds are woven into decorative mats, and rattan is used to make mats and baskets of exceptional durability. A good and well made mat is said to last up to 30 years.

Beadwork, traditional to the native people of Sabah and Sarawak, is extremely attractive when sewn onto headbands, necklaces, belts, buttons and baskets. Those available for sale in Kuala Lumpur tend to be commercial, but are still attractive souvenirs – at least the designs are native.

Much more rare is the intricate beadwork that typifies the Melaka Peranakan heritage, a blend of Malay and Chinese cultures. This finely crafted work appears on embroidered evening handbags and slippers (*manik-manik*), and feature in select local *haute couture* labels.

Gold

Gold has an allure that transcends international boundaries, but where Malaysian gold jewellery is concerned, there are four major traditions at work here, ie Malay, Western, Chinese and Indian.

Malay, Chinese and Indian goldsmiths tend to use pure gold (up to 24 karat) in fabricating jewellery, as opposed to Western jewellers who combine gold with other precious metals. Even the designs are different. Malay and Indian jewellery tends to have distinct Muslim and Hindu religious overtones, while dragon and phoenix motifs and the use of jade are common features in Chinese jewellery.

The major gold retailers in the city are Poh Kong Jewellers in The Mall, Lee Cheong Jewellers at Jalan Tun H S Lee, Abdul Razak Goldsmith at Lebuh Ampang, and international jewellers such as Selberan with outlets in Lot 10, The Mall and Yow Chuan Plaza, and P H Henry at Jalan Tuanku Abdul Rahman.

Clothing

Good quality cotton, linen and silk, either made locally or imported, are fashioned into ready-to-wear clothing. Most department stores carry their own labels, usually mostly local, and a selection of limited international brands. Most outfits are best suited to warm tropical climes of course, and large sizes can sometimes be difficult to find. However tailors are equipped to handle made-to-measure orders at fairly reasonable prices and

can sometimes deliver within 24 hours. Boutiques offer exclusive designs that can be customised for your requirements. Prices here, however, are generally higher. Malaysia has some talented fashion designers, some of whom are doing the country proud internationally, such as New York-based Zang Toi. Local designer brands are usually available as both *haute couture* and ready-to-wear, and there are some spectacular evening wear collections, some of which feature local influences.

Then there is local dress: for women this comes in the form of the *baju kurung*, the Malay long blouse and long skirt outfit, and the *kebaya*, a more body-hugging version of it; the Chinese *cheongsam*; and the Indian *sari* or *salwa khameez* trouser-suit. For men, there is the *baju Melayu*, a cotton or silk outfit with a mandarin-like collar and *sampin*, a sarung worn around the hips; the Chinese Mandarin-collared shirt; and the Indian *khurta* cotton top.

Miscellaneous

Cameras, pens, watches and mini stereo systems are relatively inexpensive as they are exempted from import duty. A wide variety is available, and retail outlets can be found in all the large shopping complexes. Imported goods, however, can be expensive. Locally made leather goods are a worthwhile buy. In fact, many leading fashion houses have their products made in Malaysia.

Where to Buy

The best Malaysian handicrafts, unfortunately, are not found in Kuala Lumpur, but in their home states. A good variety, however, can be found in the **Kompleks Budaya Kraf** on Jalan Conlay and in the shops at **Central Market**. Pewterware can be purchased in major department stores and the **Royal Selangor Pewter** showroom in Cheras, where there are factory tours too.

There are many shops that sell *batik* and *songket* in Jalan Tun Perak, and it is a good idea to check these out at the **Jalan Tuanku Abdul Rahman** and **Masjid India** areas, as well as the bazaars in **Kampung Bahru** and **Jalan Raja Laut**.

Shops in **Masjid India**, **Jalan Melayu** and **Lorong Bugus** also sell textiles, clothes, religious paraphernalia, metalware and handicrafts from countries such as India, Pakistan, the Middle East and Indonesia. Browse through these speciality shops and you will find value-for-money items.

Chinatown, naturally, is the place for Chinese and Taiwanese goods such as Chinese medicines, herbs, spices and Taoist prayer items. Equally ubiquitous in Chinatown are shops and sidewalk vendors that stock cheap clothing – albeit with fake brand names – shoes, toys, crockery and other household items. These stalls are also interspersed with sidewalk vendors from exotic destinations like Nepal and Russia, who sell a range of unusual merchandise.

For better quality and designer labels, the best bet would be the large shopping complexes. Good places to shop include **Lot 10**, **Sungei Wang Plaza**, **Bukit Bintang Plaza**, **Star Hill** and **KL Plaza** in Bukit Bintang; **Imbi Plaza** in the same area for computer and electronics buffs; **Suria KLCC**, **Ampang Park**, **Yow Chuan Plaza** and **City Square** along Jalan Ampang; **Sogo** and **Globe Silk Store** on Jalan Tuanku Abdul Rahman and **Pertama Complex** on the same road for leather and budget goods; **The Mall** on Jalan Putra; and **The Weld** on Jalan Raja Chulan. Outside of the town centre, try the **Bangsar Shopping Complex** in Bangsar, the **Mid-Valley MegaMall** close by (incidentally the largest mall in the country), **1 Utama** in Bandar Utama and **Jaya's (Section 14)** and **Subang Parade** in Petaling Jaya.

Left: an array of *songkok*
Above: a Chinatown antique dealer

EATING OUT

Kuala Lumpur is probably not the best place in the world to start dieting. The variety of food is endless, the portions large and the prices reasonable. In the end, it is probably wiser to let your epicurean urges go wild and sample what the city has to offer. You have a choice of indigenous Malay, Chinese, Indian, Nonya food, besides French, Mexican, Spanish, Italian, Japanese and Korean cuisines. Even the major cuisines have sub-types that are radically different.

With 13 states and culinary specialities within each region, the array of Malay food is almost infinite. As for Chinese food, every provincial variety is available, be it Cantonese, Hokkien, Teochew or Hainanese. Some of the dishes have become so localised they can only be labelled Malaysian, such as *bak-kut-teh*, pork stewed in a soup of five-spice powder and coriander. Nonya food is a delicious hybrid of Chinese and Malay cuisines. Indian food covers the spectrum of South Indian, Punjabi, Moghul and Indian-Muslim dishes. There are also different ways of cooking the same foods: seafood, a Malaysian favourite, can be done Chinese or Malay style, while vegetarian food has both Chinese and Indian varieties.

Open-air dining

If the range of cuisines hasn't excited your tastebuds, then perhaps the varied locations in which the food is served might. These range from fine continental restaurants to the street stalls which come alive every evening on most street corners. The quality of the food, however, has nothing to do with where it is served. Some of Kuala Lumpur's best food comes from hawkers and the locals know it. Don't fret if some of the stalls do not appear to be clean; just make sure the food is freshly cooked, and avoid ice cubes.

Hawker food is something no visitor should miss while in Kuala Lumpur. Not only do hawkers serve a variety of authentic local dishes, prices are also very reasonable and hawker-stall dining is an experience on its own. Although roadside stalls are a common sight, the modernisation of the city has swept many of these hawkers into the concrete, air-conditioned food arcades of shopping malls (see listing under *Hawker Centres* for their locations).

Open-air hawker centres are scattered all over the city and some of the larger ones are in Petaling Street (mostly Chinese food); Jalan Bunus (mainly Malay and Indonesian food); Jalan Alor (Chinese/Penang food); Brickfields (mixed local food but mainly Indian); Chow Kit (mostly Malay food); Jalan Kampung Attap, along Jalan Imbi (Chinese Malaysian); Subang Jaya (mixed); Jalan SS2 in Petaling Jaya (mixed); and Damansara Uptown, Damansara Utama, PJ (Malay and Chinese).

Food vendors also group together in shop lots on every other street. Some hawkers keep going till 2 or 3am and there are others who even keep their stalls open till dawn. Bangsar Baru stalls are particularly popu-

Above: *mee rebus*, Malay-style noodles smothered in spicy gravy

lar among the young crowds returning from a night of partying.

The list on the following pages is by no means exhaustive; entire books have been devoted to the topic. Price categories for a meal for two without drinks are categorised as:

$ = under RM30
$$ = RM30–80
$$$ = RM80 and above.

Malay
Paya Serai Restaurant
PJ Hilton
Tel: 03-7559122
Buffet selection of Malay, Chinese and Indian dishes. Good for those wary of hawker food. $$

Rasa Utara
Bukit Bintang Plaza
Jalan Bukit Bintang
Tel: 03-2488369
Specialises in northern Malay cuisine. Try the *ayam percik*, a hot and sour chicken dish which has made the state of Kelantan proud. $$

Seri Melayu
1 Jalan Conlay
Tel: 03-2451833
Located in a large wooden traditional house, the restaurant serves good Malay food accompanied by a cultural performance. $$

Nasi Lemak Benteng Utama
Jalan Bunus 1 (Masjid India area)
A dinner-only riverside stall that sells fragrant coconut milk rice with spicy dishes; try the potato cutlets, chicken curry and beef *rendang*. $

Nelayan Restaurant
Taman Tasik Titiwangsa
Tel: 03-40228400
Offering typical Malay cuisine, specialising in 'steamboat'. $

Chinese
Golden Phoenix Restaurant
Hotel Equatorial
Jalan Sultan Ismail
Tel: 03-2617777
Serves mainly Cantonese cuisine using only the freshest of ingredients. Dishes to try include the sizzling venison on hotplate, braised abalone and salt-baked prawns. $$$

Hai Tien Lo
Pan Pacific Hotel
Tel: 03-4425555
Serves excellent Cantonese and Szechuan Chinese cuisine, all *halal* (kosher). $$$

Museum Chinese Restaurant
Legend Hotel
The Mall Putra Place
Tel: 03-4429888
Fine dining in lovely ambience, with Teochew specialities including prawns and chicken. $$$

Shang Palace
Shangri-La Hotel
Jalan Sultan Ismail
Tel: 03-2322388
One of the best Chinese restaurants in the city with good *dim sum* for lunch. Recommended are the steamed pork buns. $$$

Hakka Restaurant
off Jalan Maarof, Bangsar Baru
Tel: 03-2824211
Specialises in Hakka food, which features lots of braised meat dishes. $$

Marco Polo Restaurant
1st floor, Wisma Lim Foo Yong
Jalan Raja Chulan
Tel: 03-2412233
Traditional Cantonese cuisine. Try their specialities: the steamed fish and prawn cake wrapped in bamboo shoot. $$

Ming Palace
Ming Court Vista Hotel
Jalan Ampang
Tel: 03-21618888
Try the Peking duck carved right at your table. $$

New Formosa Restaurant
46 Jalan SS 2/24, Petaling Jaya
Tel: 03-78757478
Serves Taiwanese food, known especially for steamboat – a do-it-yourself meal of raw meats and greens cooked in a boiling cauldron of rich stock. $$

Oversea Restaurant
Central Market
Tel: 03-22746407
Good Cantonese cuisine; try the pork ribs and chilly *kung pao* chicken. $$

Cosy Corner
1st floor, Ampang Park
Tel: 03-2615649
Wide variety of tasty Malaysian and Cantonese dishes. $

Esquire Kitchen
Level 1, Sungei Wang Plaza
Jalan Sultan Ismail
Tel: 03-2484506
Dumplings and pork dishes are the main draw of this centrally-located restaurant. $

South Indian
Devi's Corner Restaurant
Jalan Telawi 1, Bangsar Baru
Tel: 03-22744173
Traditional South Indian breads and rice-and-curry dishes served on a banana leaf. Best eaten with your fingers. $

Krishna Curry House
10 Jalan SS 51A/222, PJ
Tel: 03-7564920
Highly rated among knowing gourmets. Known for its spicy mutton and vegetable dishes. $

North Indian/Pakistani
Bombay Palace
388 Jalan Tun Razak
Tel: 03-2454241
In a smart bungalow with nice ambience and gracious staff. Try the royal banquet of *tandoori* or vegetarian dishes. $$$

Taj Restaurant
Crown Princess Hotel
Tel: 03-2625522
Upmarket establishment and an award-winning North Indian restaurant in KL. Live Indian music while you dine. $$$

Bangles
60A Jalan Tuanku Abdul Rahman
Tel: 03-2986770
One of the city's oldest North Indian restaurants, with kitschy decor – including bangles and mirrors. Tasty food; try the *kurmas*. $$

Gem Restaurant
Jalan Tun Sambanthan
Brickfields
Sample their *naan* bread with *masala* or *tandoori* chicken, along with their spiced tea. $$

Bilal Restaurant
33 Jalan Ampang
Tel: 03-2380804
Another very old restaurant. This began as an offshoot of the Federal Bakeries, at one time the city's largest producer of bread. $

Vegetarian
Annalakshmi Restaurant
44–46 Jalan Maarof, Bangsar Baru
Tel: 03-2823799
The city's most famous Indian vegetarian restaurant. $$

Govinda's
16–1 Lorong Bunus Enam
Tel: 03-2986785
Vedic cuisine (no meat, fish, eggs or milk) in Little India. $

Wan Fo Yuan
8 Jalan Panggung, Chinatown
Tel: 03-2380952
Good Chinese-style bean curd dishes, centrally located to Petaling Street. $

Nonya
Bon Ton Restaurant
7 Jalan Kia Peng
Tel: 03-2413614
A restaurant in a converted bungalow under raintrees. Creative Western and local dishes. $$

Left: foodstall along Jalan Masjid India

Dondang Sayang
Lower ground floor, The Weld
Tel: 03-2613831
Good for the Enche Kebin chicken, and *otak-otak* baked fish. $$

Kapitan's Club
35 Jalan Ampang
Tel: 03-2010242
Good nonya dishes. Try top hats, *ayam* Kapitan and Portugese baked fish. $$

Thai
Restoran Thaibase
32, Jalan SS 2/10
Petaling Jaya
Tel: 03-7768587
Located in a suburb, this restaurant is unsparing with chillies. Great mango salad, fried fish cake and green curry. $$

Thai Corner
12 Jalan Telawi 4
Bangsar Baru
Tel: 03-2554604
Good selection. Try the tasty green chicken curry and chicken in pandan leaf. $

Seafood
Bangsar Seafood Village
3 Jalan Telawi Empat
Lot 4387
Tel: 03-2822555
Open-air restaurant serving seafood cooked Chinese style. $$

Eden Seafood Village
Jalan Raja Chulan
Tel: 03-2414027
Part of a chain of seafood restaurants found in major towns. Local seafood as well as imported lobsters, oysters and salmon. Most of the food is cooked Western style. $$

Happy Valley Seafood Village
18 Jalan Delima, off Jalan Imbi
Tel: 03-2422625
Sample the extensive selection of Cantonese seafood dishes offered here. $$

Kelana Seafood Centre
Jalan Perbandaran
Kelana Jaya

A myriad of fresh seafood dishes for both lunch and dinner are found here. $$

Kam Ying Seafood
14 Jalan Telawi 4
Bangsar Baru
Good food at reasonable rates has made it Bangsar's most popular Chinese eatery. $

Japanese
Chikuyo-tei
Basement, Plaza See Hoy Chan
Tel: 03-2300729
One of the city's first Japanese restaurants. Quality food and fast service. $$$

Kampachi
Equatorial Hotel
Jalan Sultan Ismail
Tel: 03-2617777
Known for the quality and freshness of its food. Book ahead for Sunday buffet. $$$

Enagiku
2nd floor, Podium Block
203 Jalan Bukit Bintang
Tel: 03-2482133
Cosy Japanese-style seating restaurant. $$

Genji
PJ Hilton, 2 Jalan Barat
Tel: 03-7559122
The house specialities are California rolls and *shabu shabu*. $$

Above: cheap chillies

Western

Ciao
428, Jalan Tun Razak
(near RHB Bank)
Tel: 03-9854827
Excellent Italian pasta and pizza in a lovely bungalow setting. $$$

Flamenco
1st floor, KL Plaza
Tel: 03-2452213
Bright decor, Mediterranean food including *tapas* and *paella*. $$$

Les Tableaux
38 Jalan Walter Grenier
Tel: 03-2459504
Excellent French-Belgian cuisine; you can bring your own wine. $$$

Mahsuri
Carcosa Sri Negara
Jalan Taman Tasik Perdana
Tel: 03-2821888
Excellent high tea spread and elegant Italian dining. $$$

The Mango Tree
4 Lorong Maarof
Bangsar Utama
Tel: 03-2846268
This Western/Italian restaurant has an imaginative menu and well-presented food. $$$

Citrus
Jalan Sultan Ismail
(opposite Concorde Hotel)
Tel: 03-2425188
Specialising in so-called cross-cultural East-West cuisine. $$

Coliseum Café
98 Jalan Tuanku Abdul Rahman
Tel: 03-2926270
A historical landmark. Highly recommended is its Sunday tiffin of chicken curry. $$

Hard Rock Café
Wisma Concorde
Jalan Sultan Ismail
Tel: 03-2444062
Tested formula: rock memorabilia, American food and loud music. $$

Jake's Charbroil Steaks
21 Jalan Setiapuspa
Medan Damansara
Tel: 03-2545677
Serves good Mexican starters and is well-known for its grilled fish and steaks. $$

Modesto's
12A Jalan Telawi 3
Bangsar Baru
Tel: 03-2842445, 2842446
Also in Jalan P Ramlee. A good spread of pastas, pizzas and must-try tiramisu. $$

TGI Friday's
Ground floor Life Centre
Jalan Sultan Ismail
Tel: 03-2637761
Tex-Mex cuisine. $$

The Ship
Jalan Sultan Ismail
Tel: 03-2418805
Tasty steaks, chops, and fish and chips in a nautical setting. Several outlets in city. $$

Hawker Centres

Central Market
All types of local and fast food. Especially good are the *char kway teow* (fried flat rice noodles tossed in a spicy sweet black sauce) and *Hokkien mee*, yellow wheat noodles in a rich pork-based stock.

Food Court
Top floor, Kota Raya Shopping Complex
A good mix of local fare.

Hawker's Centre
Top floor, Sungei Wang Plaza
Mainly Malay and Chinese food.

Jalan Alur
Bukit Bintang
Authentic Penang fare all in one street.

Jalan Raja Alang
Kampung Bahru
Mainly Malay food.

Medan Hang Tuah
4th floor of The Mall
Local food sold in the setting of 1930s KL.

Right: night market scene at Jalan Petaling

NIGHTLIFE

Kuala Lumpur's nightlife is not as racy as Manila's or Bangkok's but there is still plenty of action for visitors who want to see a different side to the city. Known as the 'garden city of lights', Kuala Lumpur lives up to its name when the sun goes down. The city has a varied nightlife, with many shops open until 10pm, and an active streetlife as well. Whether it is eating and shopping, nightclubbing or pub crawling, there is enough to keep you awake till the wee hours of the morning.

Night Markets

Every day, the city authorities close off a street or two to vehicles, turning the space over to small-time traders and hawkers for the evening. The *pasar malam*, or night markets, are a hallowed institution in Malaysia. These are colourful and lively open-air bazaars whose itinerant vendors sell everything from fresh vegetables, meat, fish, fruits and cooked food, to toys, household ware, electronics, clothes and bric-a-brac.

However, it is not just the variety of merchandise that makes the night markets special for KL-ites. The markets are social institutions as well, providing an opportunity for neighbours and friends to meet in the cool of the evening. Since night markets are not necessarily set up in the same spots every evening, ask your hotel concierge for specific locations each evening. This infor-mation can also be obtained from the Tourist Information Centres. Following are some popular night market sites in the city: **Jalan Angsana**, off Jalan Tun Sambanthan on Wednesday; **Kampung Datuk Keramat** on Friday; **Jalan Tuanku Abdul Rahman**, **Jalan Telawi Dua** and **Bangsar Baru** on Saturday; and **Taman Tun Dr Ismail** on Sunday.

Lounges

Lounges are found in hotels and are often places where business deals are sealed over drinks or coffee. Lounges are also hot favourites with the older crowd and snuggling couples. Open in concept and furnished with comfortable sofas, the entertainment usually comprises easy listening music by a live band, more often than not Filipino, or a singer and pianist. One of the most popular and lively lounges is at the **Concorde Hotel** in Jalan Sultan Ismail; one of the most posh is **Shangri-la's**, across the road.

Dance Clubs

There are quite a few discos or dance clubs in Kuala Lumpur, ranging from the ultratrendy where yuppies come dressed to kill, to dark seedy bars that you wouldn't want to be caught dead in. Most good hotels have dance clubs as standard fixtures. Most are open on weekdays from 5pm–1am, with happy hours ending at around 9pm; on weekends these clubs remain open till 3am or later.

The following are recommended: TM2 at the Kuala Lumpur Hilton; **Musictheque** at the Istana; **Hard Rock Café** at the Concorde Hotel; **Roxy** at the Rennaisance Hotel; and **The Backroom** behind Shangri-La. The Golden Triangle club cluster at Jalan Sultan Ismail and Jalan P Ramlee area includes **The Emporium**, **The Beach**, **The Talk**, **Brannigan's**, **Modesto's**, and a little away in Jalan Mayang opposite the Australian High Commission, **El Nino**. In Petaling Jaya, head for hot spots like **Viva** at the Eastin Hotel in Jalan Damansara, and **Uncle Chillie's** at the PJ Hilton.

This list is by no means exhaustive. Daily newspapers and entertainment magazines like *Day and Night* carry comprehensive listings of entertainment spots around the city.

Pubs

While alcohol is not a central feature of traditional Malaysian culture, an increasing number of office workers, businessmen and executives congregate in these watering holes after work to wash down their tribulations with a beer or two before trudging home. Most pubs serve food, the mainstay being sandwiches, fried chicken wings and French fries. In addition, many pubs feature live music and almost all have sound systems, playing popular tunes.

Pubs come and go all the time but the ones with staying power include the unimaginatively-titled **The Pub** in Shangri-La Hotel and the beer garden, **Blues Café**, at Lot 10 in Bukit Bintang. **Tapas Bar** at Micasa Hotel & Apartments, serves great margaritas. Recently hip are cafés such as the **Benson & Hedges Bistro**, **TGI Friday's**, and **Coffee Bean and Tea Leaf**, all around the Golden Triangle club cluster; and wine and cigar bars such as **Little Havana** in Cangkat Raja Chulan behind the Istana Hotel.

Head out to the trendiest suburb, Bangsar Baru, for wall-to-wall pubs. This is the place to see and be seen. **Ronnie Q's**, **The Roof**, **Soleil's**, **Big Willy's** and **Finnegan's Irish Pub** are but a few of the spots that blend outdoor chic with urban cool.

Karaoke Lounges

Kuala Lumpur's – indeed, the country's – greatest nighttime passion is karaoke. Karaoke lounges here are essentially spruced up bars equipped with audio facilities that project musical lyrics and a suitable theme on a TV console while playing the instrumental background through a sophisticated hi-fi set-up. This provides the necessary environment for amateur singers to sing along in unison.

Kuala Lumpur and its suburbs are peppered with karaoke lounges, providing facilities ranging from the bare essentials, ie a microphone and sound system and little else, to luxuriously-outfitted lounges with state-of-the-art equipment.

Many restaurants also offer karaoke fa

Above: a makeshift Chinese opera at a night market

cilities, just as there are discos with karaoke rooms, such as **Uncle Chillie's** in the PJ Hilton, and the Hotel Istana's **Musictheque**. Some places even offer rooms decorated along themes; **Brannigan's** at Lorong Ampang has Victorian and Japanese theme rooms, while the Musictheque features rooms done up in regional Malaysian decor. Unlike in the West, most local karaoke patrons take their singing very seriously, and will not tolerate people making fun of their efforts. If you do not want to sing, avoid these bars.

Karaoke lounges may also offer the services of so-called 'guest relations officers' – pretty faces that offer lonely men easy conversation, join them in a drink and laugh at their jokes, however lame they may be. Overt hanky-panky is disallowed on the premises but the management generally closes an eye to whatever transactions spring up between their guest relations officers and customers after closing.

The better karaoke lounges would include ultra high-end **Club de Macao** in Rennaisance Hotel, **Songbird** on Jalan Imbi, and **Star KTV** at the Life Centre in Jalan Sultan Ismail and Bangsar Shopping Centre, Bangsar. Opening hours are 9pm–1am weekdays, and until 2am on weekends.

Music Clubs

Although Malaysians are generally musically inclined, finding places that play good live music can be difficult. The few good spots that have bands normally feature cover versions of popular hits. Although most of the places listed below feature live acts, it is wise to call ahead and check. When no bands are in attendance, the same places have deejays playing the latest dance music.

Those into jazz should visit **Riverbank** at Central Market and its branch at Phileo Damansara, Petaling Jaya (near Eastin Hotel). **Blues Café** on Lot 10 Jalan Bukit Bintang also features live jazz.

Hard Rock Café, in the Concorde Hotel, **The Emporium** down the road, and **Uncle Chillie's** in PJ Hilton sometimes feature live groups. **Blue Moon** in Equatorial Hotel plays oldies but goodies from the 1950s, while KL Hilton's **TM2** band belts out favourites from the 1960s to the 1980s.

Damansara Utama, in Petaling Jaya, has over 30 pubs, some featuring good bands.

For canto-pop (Chinese language hits), head for **Halo Café** at Jalan Balai Polis in Chinatown. The more hard core riffs can grab a drink at **Halo Rock Café** at the end of the block. These clubs are also where aspiring singers get the chance to audition, get some training in vocal and performance skills, and a chance to perform before an audience, in the hope that they get spotted by a talent agent.

Theatre

There is a small but active theatre scene in Kuala Lumpur, with plays held infrequently at the **Dewan Bandaraya** on Jalan Raja Laut, **Panggung Eksperimen** off Jalan Parlimen, **Panggung Negara**, the massive national theatre, and the **Malaysian Tourist Information Centre** (MATIC) on Jalan Ampang. The only venue that features regular acts is **The Actor's Studio** beneath Dataran Merdeka. They have two theatres here, and feature amateur performances in English, including revue, modern dance, stand-up comedy, and skits. There is a lot of interest in coming up with Malaysian artforms, whether it be localising foreign works, or incorporation Malay, Chinese or Indian elements in original productions. The results vary, but can be interesting. For details, check the dailies or with The Actor's Studio (tel: 03-294 5400, website: www.theactorsstudio.com.my) or the local arts scene website www.kulture.com.my.

Cultural shows are also held occasionally at **Central Market**, usually for free. Some restaurants also feature local dance performances of the commercial variety. Among them is **Sri Melayu** in Jalan Conlay and **Restoran Nelayan** next to Lake Titwangsa behind the National Theatre. The top classical concert venue is the **Dewan Filharmonik Petronas** theatre in the KLCC (tel: 03-207 7007, 10am–6pm, website: www.petronas.com.my/dfp/dfpmain.htm).

There is a full and interesting programme of performances by the resident philharmonic orchestra all year round. Occasionally, guest artistes appear with the orchestra and the Petronas Dance Troupe have scheduled performances too.

CALENDAR OF EVENTS

The multi-ethnic mix in Malaysia – a blend of Malays, Chinese, Indians, Eurasians and at least 30 other indigenous and other ethnic groups – weaves a social fabric embroidered with tradition, variety and colour. Auspicious occasions and festivals of religious and cultural significance of each group take place throughout the year, in consonance with different calendar systems.

Malaysians observe an 'open house' tradition during these festivities, inviting friends and relatives to their homes for social visits and to indulge in that great Malaysian pastime – eating.

A good many festival dates are not fixed as they shift annually, depending on the lunar and Muslim calendars. Check with Tourist Information Centres for the exact dates of celebrations.

January/February

Thaipusam (January/February): Commemorates the handing over of the *vale* (trident) of virtue to the Hindu deity, Lord Subramaniam. It is celebrated by Hindus all over the country with great fervour. Thousands converge at one of the holiest Hindu shrines at Batu Caves to offer thanks and pray, many of them bearing *kavadi*, a wooden framed structure designed to carry containers of milk and rose water, as offerings. Sometimes the procession takes on a macabre dimension, with skewers pierced into the bodies of the *kavadi* bearers. The crowds start gathering the evening before when the statue of Lord Subramaniam is drawn by chariot from the Sri Mahamariamman Temple on Jalan Bandar to the temple cave. *Kavadi*-bearers generally begin their 272-step climb at dawn, but devotees throng the temple the whole day.

Federal Territory Day (February 1): Kuala Lumpur brings out the fireworks, streamers and balloons to celebrate its birthday. Special events, from cultural and musical performances to watersports, take place throughout the day.

Chinese New Year (January/February): This important Chinese festival heralds the first moon of the lunar new year, and is marked by prayers, reunion dinners and lion dances. Although only two days are designated as public holidays, most Chinese owned shops close for up to five days. Chinatown is at its best before the celebration. Join the crowds in their last-minute shopping on the eve at Jalan Petaling and try the festive goodies, many of which are imported from China.

May/June

Wesak Day (May/June): The most significant festival for Buddhists commemorates the birth, enlightenment and death of Lord Buddha. Temples are packed with devotees offering prayers and giving alms to the monks. Visit the International Buddhist Pagoda along Jalan Berhala, Brickfields, or the temple off Jalan Gasing in Petaling Jaya. The air is usually thick with the smell and smoke from giant joss-sticks on the temple grounds, compounded by that from the hundreds of joss-sticks raised in prayer by constant streams of devotees to the statue of Lord Buddha and other deities. Worshippers receive yellow strings from the monks to be worn around their wrists for luck.

August

Merdeka Day (August 31): Malaysia's Hari Kebangsaan (National Day) is celebrated with a mammoth parade at Dataran Merdeka along Jalan Raja; with processions of floats representing all the states. Here, in 1957, the declaration of independence was made. The parade starts early at around 7 or 8am and is difficult to view unless you go to the

Left: Chinese New Year festivities

square very early. Alternatively, watch it on TV. Roads in the immediate vicinity are closed to traffic.

September
Malaysia Fest (September): A lavish two-week fete of regional festivities, foods and handicrafts held in hotels and large shopping complexes in Kuala Lumpur.

Mooncake or **Lantern Festival** (September): This is a Chinese festival to celebrate the overthrowing of the Mongolian Dynasty by the people in China. Messages hidden in specially baked mooncakes were supposed to have helped fuel the revolution. Traditionally filled with sesame seed paste and egg, modern moon cakes now have a variety of fillings, including green *pandan* (screwpine leaves) and even the stinky durian fruit. In the evening, children play with festive lanterns while women pray to the Goddess of the Moon.

Festival of the Hungry Ghost (September): Altars with tiny teacups and food as well as candles on street corners and pavements are the most visible signs of this Chinese celebration. The Chinese believe that during this seventh month of the lunar calendar, the gates of hell open and souls in purgatory wander the earth, and must therefore be appeased with the offering of food. Joss sticks and 'hell money' are sometimes burned. This is believed to be an unlucky month to get married or move homes.

October/November
Deepavali (October/November): Also known as the Festival of Lights, this falls in the Tamil month of Aipassi. Hindus celebrate the triumph of light over darkness and good over evil with prayers, and line their gardens with oil lamps to receive blessings from Lakshmi, the Goddess of Wealth. Another 'open house' affair.

December
Christmas (December 25) is celebrated with imitation fir trees, carolling in shopping malls, and midnight masses in churches. Shopping complexes and hotels take the lead with their decorations, complete with sleighs.

Variable Dates
Hari Raya Puasa: Celebrates the first day of the Muslim month of Shawal, following a month of strict fasting and prayers known as Ramadan. The start of the fasting period is governed by the Muslim calendar. Muslims usher in Hari Raya Puasa by attending prayers, followed with 'open house' the whole day long, for guests to feast on delicious home-cooked Malay food, cakes and cookies.

Hari Raya Haji, a Muslim festival celebrating the haj or religious pilgrimage to Mecca. This is a quieter affair than Hari Raya Puasa, with prayers, and the slaughtering of cows and sheep. **Maal Hijrah** is the Mulsim New Year, another sober religious celebration at mosques. Quran recitals are also held.

Above: Thaipusam devotee at Batu Caves

Practical *Information*

GETTING THERE

By Rail

The main train line from Singapore to Bangkok and beyond passes through the Stesen Keretapi Kuala Lumpur (Kuala Lumpur Railway Station). The KTM Berhad trains are modern and the service is efficient. Travellers generally take the express services, which are faster because they make a minimal number of stops. There are three classes of service. Most trains are air-conditioned and have buffet cars serving simple meals. Videos keep most passengers entertained but can be disturbing to those who want to sleep, read or simply enjoy the scenery. Sleeping berths are available on long distance trains. These are a comfortable and cheap source of accommodation for those on a budget.

There are day and night trains to both Singapore and Butterworth in Penang. From Butterworth, there are train connections to the north into Thailand. For more information, call 03-273 8000.

Several times weekly, the luxurious rail service **Eastern & Oriental Express** makes a brief, late night stop at the Railway Station. Completely refurbished to the tune of US$30 million, the train is an attempt to recreate rail travel of a bygone era. The cream-and-green coloured trains carry up to 130 passengers from Singapore to Kuala Lumpur and Butterworth, terminating in Bangkok (and vice versa). Passengers may embark at any of these points. Whatever route you decide on, rest assured it will burn a huge hole in your pockets. For reservations call: Malaysia tel: 03-781 1337, Singapore tel: 5-323 4390, Thailand tel: 662-216 5939.

By Sea

Kuala Lumpur's closest seaport is Pelabuhan Klang (Port Klang), about 40km (25 miles) away, and linked to it by highways, buses and the KTM Komuter electric train service. Ferries from Sumatra, Indonesia, dock here; smaller ferries travel daily here from Tanjong Balai near Medan. Port Klang is the main port of call for regional cruise ships, and less regularly, the international liners.

By Road

The North-South highway from Singapore to the Thai border provides a convenient means of travel through Peninsular Malaysia, the entire trip taking about 12 hours by car one way. There are two links from Singapore: across the Causeway from Woodlands to Johor Bahru, and Linke Dua (Second Link) from Tuas to Tanjung Kupang. Try and avoid crossing the border on Friday afternoons and during public holidays because of the traffic congestion at the checkpoints.

Long distance buses and taxis also travel to and from Kuala Lumpur to most destinations on the peninsula as well as Singapore and Thailand. The interstate bus stations are at Puduraya near Chinatown, and Putra and Hentian Pekeliling near The Mall. Long distance air-conditioned express buses are fast, economical and comfortable, with video entertainment on board. The buses make occasional half-hour stops for drinks, meals and toilet breaks.

Long distance taxis also leave from Puduraya. Share the cost with three other passengers, or if you are in a hurry or don't want to travel with strangers, pay for the whole taxi. Most 'teksi' are diesel-powered Mercedes and have air-conditioning.

eft: KL Railway Station at night
ight: North-South Highway

By Air

The Kuala Lumpur International Airport (KLIA) is located 70km (43 miles) south of the city in Sepang and is one of Asia's biggest and most modern airports. Planes arrive and depart from four satellite arms, which are linked to the main terminal building via an aerotrain. Domestic flights operate from the Sultan Abdul Aziz Shah Airport in Subang, except for selected sectors with international connections.

KLIA houses the national carrier **Malaysia Airlines (MAS)**, tel: 03-746 3000 (24 hours), which provides both international and domestic connections to destinations on the peninsula and east Malaysia. MAS flies to and from every continent except Antarctica.

Other domestic carriers include **Pelangi Air**, **Berjaya Air** and **Air Asia**. Some domestic services fly out of the Sultan Abdul Aziz Shah Airport in Subang, (also known as the Subang Airport) about 30 minutes from the city centre. Internal airfares are set by the government but cheaper international fares can be negotiated with travel agents. Kuala Lumpur is reputed to be a good place to buy cheap international fares. In addition to MAS, Kuala Lumpur is also well-connected by international carriers.

MAS has discounted fares on some domestic flights but this means travelling at inconvenient times. If interested you should ask for their 'night tourist fares'. Discounted student and group fares (minimum three) are also available. Note: All domestic and international flights on MAS, except those to Japan, are non-smoking.

Departure tax on international flights is RM40 while that of domestic flights is RM10. Tickets purchased in Malaysia will include the tax, while those purchased outside the country, probably will not. If so, you may pay the tax at the check-in counter.

Arriving in Kuala Lumpur on an international flight is easy, with all signs in both Bahasa Malaysia and English. You have to declare how much money you bring into and out of the country. Note that possession of drugs is a capital offence.

For the airport limousine service, buy a coupon with fixed fares for your destination but this is expensive if you're alone (toll-free tel: 1-800-880 737). Buses depart from the basement every 15 minutes to Hentian Duta, one hour away, from where you can catch a bus or taxi to town. Buses also go to the Subang Jaya (every one hour) and Nilai KTM commuter train stations (every 30 minutes) where you can catch a train into town. Accommodation and car hire facilities are also available at the airport. City taxis cannot legally pick up passengers at the airport, but you can catch any taxi from the city to the airport – the fare is based on mileage plus a surcharge.

TRAVEL ESSENTIALS

When to Visit

Kuala Lumpur is hot and humid. Daytime temperatures can reach a high of 33°C (91°F) while the nights can be balmy, with the temperature dropping by as much as 10°C (18°F), although most times, the difference is slight. Humidity is almost always above 80 percent. As the city has no defined seasonal weather patterns, a visit can be planned for any time of the year. The central mountain range keeps out the worst of the northeast monsoon (November–February), and the city's inland location protects it from the south-west monsoon (July–September).

Kuala Lumpur gets its share of heavy rain though, with downpours and flash floods mostly in the afternoon and early evening.

Visas

Visa requirements change, so check with the relevant Malaysian embassy/consulate before travelling. At time of press, citizens of the Commonwealth and ASEAN, Ireland, Switzerland, the Netherlands, San Marino and Liechtenstein do not need a visa to visit.

The following nationals do not need a visa for a visit not exceeding three months: Austria, Australia, Belgium, Italy, Japan, South Korea, Tunisia, the United States, Germany, France, Norway, Sweden, Denmark, Belgium, Finland, Luxembourg and Iceland. Citizens of Bulgaria, Rumania, Russia (CIS) and Yugoslavia are allowed a seven-day visa-free visit.

Immigration requests that travellers have passports that are valid for at least six months at time of entry.

Tourist visas may be extended by applying at the **Immigration Department**, Block 1, Pusat Bandar Damansara, Damansara Heights (tel: 03-255 5077; Monday–Friday 8am–4.15pm, Saturday 8am –12.45pm).

Vaccinations

A yellow fever vaccination is required if arriving from an infected country.

Clothing

Clothes should be light and loose so pack cottons and natural fibres, instead of synthetics. Sunglasses, sun block and umbrellas are advisable. Shoes should be removed before entering temples and homes, so slip-ons are handy.

Electricity

Power supply is 220 or 240 volts at 50 Hz cycle. Most outlets use the three-pin, flat-pronged plugs and many hotels have 110-volt shaving sockets.

Time Differences

Kuala Lumpur is 8 hours ahead of GMT and 16 hours ahead of US Pacific Standard Time.

GETTING ACQUAINTED

Geography and Population

Malaysia's land mass of 330,434sq km (127,580sq miles) covers the Malay Peninsula and a third of Borneo. It is one of the world's largest exporters of rubber and palm oil, and produces substantial amounts of petroleum, pepper and tropical hardwoods. On the manufacturing side, the country is also the world's largest exporter of semi-conductors, rubber gloves and condoms, and the second largest exporter of air-conditioners.

Kuala Lumpur, the nation's capital, is situated about halfway down the west coast of the peninsula and 35km (22 miles) inland. Dubbed Malaysia's Garden City of Lights, it started as a riverine trading post at the confluence of the Klang and Gombak rivers over a century ago. Kuala Lumpur has since grown to a metropolis with an area of about 234sq km (90sq miles) populated by over 2 million inhabitants.

Malaysia's 21-million population comprises mostly indigenous Malays, Dayaks, Muruts, Bidayuhs, Kadazans, Orang Asli and about 30 other cultures of Melano-Polynesian stock (making up 60 percent of the population), followed by substantial numbers of Chinese and Indians as well as smaller numbers of Portuguese, Eurasians and others. The Chinese largely belong to the Cantonese, Hokkien and Hakka dialect groups. The Indians consist mainly of Tamils, followed by significant numbers of Malayalis, Punjabis and Sindhis.

Government and Economy

As an ex-British colony, Malaysia's legal and economic systems trace their origins to England. Although the sultan of each state still plays a role within the country, this role is becoming increasingly ceremonial. The political system is a constitutional monarchy with the King, or the Yang di-Pertuan Agong, elected every five years on a rotational basis by the 11 peninsular state rulers. The current Yang Di-Pertuan Agong is also the Sultan of Selangor.

Malaysia comprises 13 states located on the peninsula along with Sarawak and Sabah in East Malaysia on the island of Borneo. In addition, there is the Federal Territory comprising Kuala Lumpur and the international offshore financial centre of Labuan.

There are two houses of parliament; the lower house or Dewan Rakyat, and the senate or Dewan Negara. Some of the latter are appointed by the Yang di-Pertuan Agong while others are elected by the legislatures of individual states. Members are elected every five years and the current government is a coalition of Barisan National parties with Dato' Seri Dr Mahathir Mohamad as Prime Minister. State governments are elected for

Above: Indians are a minority race

the same period of office but there is no upper house.

Before the Asian economic meltdown in 1997, Malaysia's GNP growth averaged 8 percent for a decade. The Tiger Nation was well on its way to achieving its goal of developed nation status by 2020. The major shift from agriculture to manufacturing pushed the country into the top 20 largest trading nations in the world. The devaluation of the ringgit and the loss of two-thirds of its market capitalisation, however, has dented some of its ambition. The economy is on the recovery somewhat, with a modest 4 percent GDP growth in 1999.

Unemployment remains low although inflation is climbing, and economic resuscitation includes stabilising the ringgit and stimulating both domestic and external demand for Malaysian-produced goods. A key investment-attracting tool is the ambitious information technology-based Multimedia Super Corridor (MSC) project in Selangor. Malaysia's main exports are electrical and electronic goods, manufactured goods, textiles, clothing and footwear, palm oil, natural gas and petroleum.

How Not to Offend

Shoes should be removed before entering a Malaysian home or place of worship. When in a mosque, visitors who are inappropriately dressed should put on a robe, which will be provided, and cover their limbs. Women should avoid wearing short skirts or shorts and should cover their heads with a scarf.

Pointing with the forefinger, pointing your feet at a person or touching a person's head is considered rude.

MONEY MATTERS

The Malaysian dollar is the ringgit (abbreviated to RM), which is worth 100 sen. Bank notes come in several denominations: RM2 (purple), RM5 (green), RM10 (red), RM20 (brownish-orange), RM50 (bluish-green), and RM100 (purple). Coins come in denominations of RM1 and 50, 20, 10, 5 and 1 sen.

Aside from everyday usage, coins are specifically needed for public phones (at 10 sen per local call), driver-operated ticket dispensers in public buses and vending machines for train and monorail tickets.

The ringgit was fixed at RM3.80 to US$1 at press time. Due to currency control regulations imposed in 1998, the ringgit cannot be traded outside the country.

Money changers can be found all over the city. Although rates vary, they offer better exchange rates than banks.

Traveller's cheques are accepted at major hotels, restaurants and department stores, although banks will give you the best rates.

Credit cards such as American Express, Diner's Club, MasterCard and Visa are widely accepted by most establishments throughout Kuala Lumpur. Note that retail shops may impose a 2–5 percent surcharge if you pay for your shopping by credit card.

Tipping

Large service establishments such as hotels, restaurants, bars and clubs add a service charge automatically to bills, so tipping is not necessary. However, whenever good service is rendered, a small tip will be much appreciated. Taxis generally expect the exact meter fare.

GETTING AROUND

Taxis

Kuala Lumpur is well served by a system of highways which bring commuters, taxis, buses and cars into the centre of the city. While traffic jams have not yet reached Bangkok's disastrous gridlocks, they are well on the way.

Kuala Lumpur's taxis are conspicuously painted yellow and black or red and white. They offer a convenient and economical

Right: taxi stand

means of moving around the city, and drivers usually speak at least a smattering of English. Taxi drivers are proud of their credibility and occasionally make headlines with acts of honesty. Once befriended, they can make charming conversationalists and good sources of information.

Air-conditioning and fare meters are compulsory in all taxis. Make sure the meter is activated only after you get in. Rates are RM2 for the first 2km (1.24 miles) and 10 sen for each additional 200m (½ mile). There is a surcharge of RM1 for booking a taxi by phone. There is also a 50 percent surcharge on the meter fare between midnight and 6am. If there are more than two passengers per taxi, 20 sen per additional passenger is levied. Hourly rates vary, some charge RM15 per hour, others add RM10 to the meter. City taxis cannot legally pick passengers up at the airport.

It is fairly easy to get a taxi either by queueing at taxi stands, flagging one down by the street, or booking one by telephone. Try to avoid hailing one between 3pm and 3.30pm, as taxi drivers change shifts around this time and usually do not pick up passengers unless you are going their way. Note: It will also be difficult to get a taxi in heavily jammed areas during rush hours.

Taxi coupons at fixed rates are available on arrival at the Kuala Lumpur International Airport. These coupons are necessary in order to take an airport limousine to the city or suburbs, and should be handed to the driver at the start of journey. The same system applies at the rail station, where tickets are sold near Platform 4.

Buses

There are several buses to choose from in Kuala Lumpur. City bus companies include Sri Jaya, Len Seng, Len Foh Hup, Toong Foong and Intrakota (air-conditioned). Aircon buses are 50 sen for the first 2km (1.24 miles) and then 5 sen per km (½ mile).

The main inner city bus stops are Puduraya, the Klang Bus Station near Chinatown, Bangkok Bank behind Central Market, Lebuh Ampang, and the Jalan Tuanku Abdul Rahman/Jalan Ipoh intersection in Chow Kit. Buses can be packed like sardine cans during peak periods, so watch your wallets.

Rental Cars

For seeing the city in style, opt for a chauffered limousine offered by a number of local car-rental companies, includng Avis, Budget, Hertz and National. Most hotels also provide air-conditioned limo services, but they tend to be more expensive.

For self-drive cars, rental rates vary according to insurance options and type of vehicle, so it is best to call around and enquire first. Payment by credit cards are preferred.

Train and Light Rail

KTM Berhad also administers the Rawang to Klang KTM Komuter electrified commuter rail service, which transports commuters and travellers within greater Kuala Lumpur and the Klang Valley.

Within the city, the Light Rail Transport (LRT) is an integrated monorail system operated by two concessionaires, Putra and Star. Air-conditioned and very convenient, the LRT services areas such as Jalan Ampang, Chow Kit, Petaling Jaya, and Bangsar. Feeder buses go to suburbs and shopping centres. Ask for maps at any station.

Maps

Tourism Malaysia (tel: 03-293 5188) has several free maps and guides covering various aspects of the city available from its information counters and in most hotels. The maps show routes, landmarks and commuter train and LRT stops within the city.

You can also get maps and more information from the Malaysian Tourist Information Complex (MATIC) at 109 Jalan Ampang; tel: 03-264 3929.

HOURS & HOLIDAYS

Business Hours

Business hours are from 8.30am or 9am to 5pm, Monday to Friday. Many businesses are also open on Saturday from 8.30 or 9am, closing by 12.30pm or 1pm. Government offices are open Monday to Friday 8am–4.15pm, and Saturday 8am–12.45pm. There is a long lunch break on Friday from 12.45pm to 2.45pm for Friday Muslim prayers.

Banks are open Monday to Friday 10am–3pm, and Saturday 9.30am–11.30pm. Post offices open Monday to Saturday 8am–4.30pm, while a handful in large housing estates are open until 10pm. The General Post Office at Menara Dayabumi, Jalan Sultan Hishamuddin, has longer opening hours. The first and third Saturday of the month is a government and banking off-day. Hotels will mail letters and sell stamps at the reception desk. Almost all department stores, supermarkets and shopping complexes are open daily from 10am to 10pm. Otherwise, shops close earlier, between 6.30–7.30pm and on Sunday.

Public Holidays

Following are official public holidays in Kuala Lumpur. Dates of ethnic festivals vary; they are determined by various lunar calendars. Check precise dates with Tourism Malaysia:

New Year's Day: January 1
Federal Territory Day: February 1
Chinese New Year: January/February
Hari Raya Puasa: Date varies
Labour Day: May 1
Wesak Day: May/June
HM the King's Birthday: June 5
Hari Raya Haji: Date varies
National Day: August 31
Prophet Muhammad's Birthday: Date varies
Deepavali: October/November
Christmas Day: December 25

ACCOMMODATION

Hotels

There is a glut of hotel rooms, which means that quality accommodation is more than affordable. Do not hesitate to negotiate for better rates than what is quoted. Hotels are all air-conditioned and complemented by restaurants and bars. Five-star hotels have swimming pools, fitness centres, shops and other facilities. Rack rates for standard double rooms are divided into five approximate price ranges:

$ = below RM100
$$ = RM100–199
$$$ = RM200–299
$$$$ = RM300–399
$$$$$ = above RM400;

Carcosa Seri Negara
Taman Tasik Perdana
Tel: 03-282 1888; Fax: 03-282 7888
Email: carcosa@mol.net.my
Immaculate all-suite hotel housed in a former Governor-General's residence and set in a private park. Its 13 suites come with private butler service. $$$$$

Chamtan Hotel
62 Jalan Masjid India
Tel: 03-293 0144; Fax: 03-293 2422
In the heart of Little India and surrounded by excellent shopping, though entertainment options are limited. $

City Hotel
366 Jalan Raja Laut
Tel: 03-4041 4466; Fax: 03-4041 5379
A reasonably-priced establishment near the Chow Kit area, which has a rather sleazy reputation. $

Concorde
2 Jalan Sultan Ismail
Tel: 03-244 2200; Fax: 03-244 1628
Email: chkl@ppp.nasionet.net
Not far from the shopping district and close to trendy restaurants and nightlife spots. Also houses the popular Hard Rock Café. $$$

Crown Princess
Jalan Tun Razak
Tel: 03-262 5522; Fax: 03-262 4687
Email: crownprincess@shikl.com
A well-appointed hotel, located next to KL's major shopping malls. Over 500 rooms and an award-winning Indian restaurant. $$$

Equatorial
Jalan Sultan Ismail
Tel: 03-2161 7777; Fax: 03-2161 7920
Email: info@eqkl.com.my
Located in the business district near shops and entertainment. $$$

Federal
35 Jalan Bukit Bintang
Tel: 03-248 9166; Fax: 03-248 2877
Email: fedhot@po.jaring.my
One of Kuala Lumpur's original hotels in the heart of Bukit Bintang. It has a revolving restaurant. $$$

Fortuna
87 Jalan Berangan
Tel: 03-241 9111; Fax: 03-241 8237
Email: fortuna@po.jaring.my
Small but central; in a quiet area behind the main Bukit Bintang area. $$

Grand Continental
Jalan Raja Laut
Tel: 03-293 9333; Fax: 03-293 9732
Email: hgckl@pd.jaring.my
Located near the Jalan Tuanku Abdul Rahman shopping area. $$

Hotel Nikko Kuala Lumpur
165 Jalan Ampang
Tel: 03-261 1111; Fax: 03-261 1122
Email: reservation@hotelnikko.com.my
A 470-room hotel with clean Japanese lines, close to the new KL City Centre. Has a popular Japanese restaurant on its premises. $$$$

Istana
Jalan Raja Chulan
Tel: 03-241 9988; Fax: 03-244 0111
Email: hotel_histana@histana.po.my
A 516-room hotel, centrally located to business and shops. Good Italian restaurant and a bar overlooking a landscaped garden. $$$

JW Marriott
Star Hill Centre, 181 Jalan Bukit Bintang
Tel: 03-2715 9000; Fax: 03-2715 7000
Website: www.marriotthotel.com
An upmarket and quietly sophisticated hotel, situated close to all the major shopping centres. $$$$

Kuala Lumpur Hilton
Jalan Sultan Ismail
Tel: 03-248 2322; Fax: 03-244 2157
Email: klhilton@tm.net.my
Recently refurbished and well-known for its dance club, TM2. Walking distance of the Bukit Bintang shops. $$$$

Kuala Lumpur Parkroyal
54 Jalan Sultan Ismail
Tel: 03-242 5588; Fax: 03-241 4281
Email: sales@prkl.com.my
A well-located property in the heart of the shopping district. $$$$

Right: plush Shangri-La Hotel

Malaya
Jalan Hang Lekir
Tel: 03-232 7722; Fax: 03-230 0980
In central Chinatown, surrounded by lots of shopping areas. $$

Mandarin
2 Jalan Sultan
Tel: 03-230 3000; Fax: 03-230 4363
Also in the heart of Chinatown, close to major bus and taxi terminals and the Central Market cultural centre. $$

Mandarin Oriental
Kuala Lumpur City Centre
Tel: 03-380 8888; Fax: 03-380-8833
Website: www.mandarin_oriental.com
Luxury accommodations next to the world's tallest twin buildings. Six restaurants, including one serving Cantonese seafood. $$$$$

Melia Kuala Lumpur
16 Jalan Imbi
Tel: 03-242 8333; Fax: 03-242 6623
Email: melia@meliakl.po.my
Quality accommodations only a short distance from the entertainment hub of Bukit Bintang. $$$$

Micasa Hotel Apartments
368B Jalan Tun Razak

Tel: 03-2161 8833; Fax: 02-2161 1186
Website: www.micasahotel.com
The city's first all-suite hotel. Rooms have
equipped kitchenettes. $$$$$

Ming Court Vista Hotel
Lot 2, Section 43
Jalan Ampang
Tel: 03-261 8888; Fax: 03-261 2393/262 3428
Email: minvista@tm.net.my
Located opposite the KLCC. A comfortable
hotel catering to a largely business traveller
clientele. $$$$

Pan Pacific
Jalan Putra
Tel: 03-442 5555; Fax: 03-443 8717
Website: www.panpac.com
Starting to show its age but with a good location; near the Putra World Trade Centre
and The Mall. Ride the glass elevator
perched outside the building for grand views
of the city. $$$$

Rennaisance Hotel/New World Hotel
Cnr Jalan Sultan Ismail/Jalan Ampang
Tel: 03-262 2233/263 6888; Fax: 03-263 1122
Website: www.rennaisance_kul.com
European-themed pair of business hotels at
the tip of the Golden Triangle. $$$$$/$$$$

Shangri-La
11 Jalan Sultan Ismail
Tel: 03-232 2388; Fax: 03-230 1514
Website: www.shangrila.com
Stylish hotel that is centrally located in the
business district and famed for its cuisine.
One of the best addresses in the city. $$$$$

Swiss Inn
Jalan Sultan
Tel: 03-232 3333; Fax: 03-241 5555
Popular hotel located in the heart of China-
town. Its sidewalk café attracts people-
watchers. $$

The Legend
Jalan Putra
Tel: 03-4042 9888; Fax: 03-4043 0700
Email: tlegend@po.jaring.my
Part of the Legend chain of hotels in Malaysia
and ideally located next to The Mall and op-
posite the Putra World Trade Centre. $$$$

The Regent Kuala Lumpur
160 Jalan Bukit Bintang
Tel: 03-241 8000; Fax: 03-242 1441
Website: www.fourseasons.com
A polished establishment with elegant
rooms, excellent service and restaurants.
Conveniently located at the fringe of Bukit
Bintang. $$$$$

Youth Hostels
KL International Youth Hostel
Jalan Kampung Attap
Tel: 03-2273 6870; Fax: 03-2274 1115
Within walking distance of Chinatown and
major bus terminals. $

YMCA
95 Jalan Padang, Brickfields
Tel: 03-2274 1439; Fax: 03-2274 0559
Near the town centre, easily accessible by
public transport. $

Guest Houses

Many small hotels housed above shop units
can be found in the city, especially along
Jalan Tuanku Abdul Rahman and in the
Chow Kit and Bukit Bintang areas. Better
known by their Malay name, rumah tumpan-
gan (lodging houses), some of them are quite
reputable. For example, the Merdeka Hotel
in Jalan Raja Muda offers decent rooms at
low prices; rates range from RM40–55.

HEALTH & EMERGENCIES
Hygiene
Drink only boiled water and bottled or
canned drinks. If you have a very sensitive
stomach, avoid ice cubes, especially in
streetside stalls and small coffeeshops, as
the ice cubes here are usually made using
unboiled water. Restaurants and other eating
places offer boiled water. Mineral and bottled water is also widely available. Food
served in licensed restaurants and at hawker
stalls is mostly clean. Regular customers are
very important for hawker stalls so most try
and keep their stalls and utensils clean.
   Pharmacies are found in most shopping
complexes. They are well-stocked and have
registered pharmacists. Controlled drugs are
sold only by prescription.

Hospitals

Many hotels have doctors on call to treat emergencies. Kuala Lumpur has a number of hospitals offering good medical care. Both government and private hospitals have fully-equipped emergency and intensive care units to cope with any medical crisis.

The **General Hospital** is at Jalan Pahang, tel: 03-292 1044, and the **Universiti Hospital** is at Jalan Universiti in suburban Petaling Jaya; its emergency ward can be contacted at tel: 03-756 4422 ext 2500. They are both government-owned hospitals.

Private hospitals include: **Tawakal Specialist Centre**, 202-A Jalan Pahang, tel: 03-423 3599; **CMH Medical Centre**, 106 Jalan Pudu, tel: 03-238 2055; **Pantai Medical Centre**, 8 Jalan Bukit Pantai, tel: 03-282 5077; **Subang Medical Centre**, 1 Jalan SS12/1A Subang Jaya, tel: 03-734 1212.

Medical and Dental Clinics

There are many 24-hour polyclinics, and privately-owned specialist clinics, which offer treatment in the city. Registered medical practitioners and qualified dental surgeons are listed in the Yellow Pages of the telephone directory.

Police Emergencies

The emergency number for police is 999, ambulance is 911 and fire is 994.

Emergency Repairs

Sidewalk cobblers and key grinders are found on almost every other downtown street and in shopping complexes. They do a pretty good job at fairly low prices. Some of them also make rubber stamps and signs.

COMMUNICATIONS & NEWS

Telecommunications

Telephone, telegram, mail, telex and fax facilities are offered by most hotels, and in the case of medium-budget to luxury hotels, IDD (international direct dial) phones are available in guest rooms. To call abroad directly, first dial the international access code 00, followed by the country code: Australia (61); France (33); Germany (49); Italy (39); Japan (81); Netherlands (31); Spain (34); UK (441); US and Canada (1).

To call Kuala Lumpur from overseas, dial the international country code 60 for Malaysia, followed by 3, the area code for Kuala Lumpur.

International calls can be made at any Kedai Telekom (Telecoms shops) located in the city during office hours. A 24-hour service is available at the Central Telekom Building in Jalan Raja Chulan. IDD pay phones are also available in popular locations. They accept most major credit cards.

The cost of a local call through a public payphone is 10 sen. Payphones maintained at shops and restaurants charge twice or three times that amount. Calls may also be made using pre-paid phone cards. These cards, sold in denominations of RM5, RM10 and RM20, are very convenient and can be purchased at selected stores such as 7-Eleven and newsstands. Payphones using these phone cards are usually in better working order since they are less prone to vandalism.

Note, however, that payphones are maintained by three companies, Uniphone, Citiphone and Telekom Malaysia, and that the various phone cards are not interchangeable.

Internet cafés are found everywhere, particularly in shopping centres, and charges range from RM4–10 per hour.

Shipping

Larger shops will handle documentation and shipping for purchases, or will recommend handling agents to do the job.

Stationery shops and some post offices sell boxes for goods to be sent by mail.

Right: a public telephone booth

News Media

There are several English dailies in Peninsular Malaysia: *The Star* and *The Sun* (morning tabloids), *The New Straits Times* (morning broadsheet), *Business Times* and *Malay Mail* (afternoon tabloid). The two largest selling, *The Star* and *The New Straits Times*, offer comprehensive coverage of local and foreign news. The *Asian Wall Street Journal, International Herald Tribune* and *USA Today* can be obtained at most newsstands and bookshops. Some shops offer other international publications too. Leading international periodicals are available at large bookshops and hotel news sellers.

Cable TV is available in most hotels, including CNN, CNBC and HBO. The specialist hotel programme packager is Vision 4. Free-to-air local TV stations are those run by state-owned Radio Televisyen Malaysia (RTM), and private stations TV3 and NTV7. All air local news reports, including in English, and American mini series and comedies alongside religious Islamic programmes.

Radio Ibu Kota (Voice of the Capital City) is a 24-hour special service for Kuala Lumpur and has programmes for visitors and travellers. It is broadcast by RTM on 97.2 MHz. FM radio has a range of English-language musical programmes from classical to jazz and pop. RTM also broadcasts an English service, Radio Four Network, from 6am to 12am. English-language news bulletins are broadcast hourly. Flip through the stations and you will hear everything from canto-pop to Hindi movie film hits and Malay rock tunes. The most 'hip' private radio stations are Hitz FM and Mix FM.

SPORTS

Swimming

Almost all hotels charging RM200 and above have swimming pools.

Public pools at **Bangsar Sports Complex** (tel: 03-282 4084); **Chin Woo Stadium** (tel: 03-232 4602); **Club Syabas** (tel: 03-757 3322); are open from 8am to midnight.

In addition, there is a massive water theme park in Bandar Sunway called the **Sunway Lagoon** (tel: 03-735 6000). It is open from noon to 7.30pm, closed Tuesday.

Jogging

Taman Tasik Perdana (Lake Gardens), **Taman Tasik Titiwangsa** off Jalan Tun Razak, **Taman Tasik Permaisuri** in Cheras, **Taman Tunku Abdul Rahman**, and the **KLCC Park** have jogging paths.

Gym and Fitness Centres

Many hotels have fully-equipped fitness centres or gyms. Also try the Weld, Wisma HLA and PJ Hilton.

Court and Racquet Games

Sports complexes in and around the city offer facilities for badminton, tennis, squash, volleyball, table tennis and *sepak takraw* (a local ball game). Courts are open from 7am or 8am till 11pm or midnight: **Bangsar Sports Complex** (tel: 03-282 4084); **Kampung Datuk Keramat** (tel: 03-456 4853); **Taman Tasik Titiwangsa** (tel: 03-423 9558); **Bandar Tun Razak Sports Complex** (tel: 03-930 8935); and **National Sports Council Complex** (tel: 03-958 1390).

Bowling

Bowling alleys can be found at: **Federal Hotel**, Jalan Bukit Bintang, **Wisma Mirama** on the 5th floor and **Yow Chuan Plaza**, Jalan Tun Razak.

Golf

Malaysia is often called a golfer's paradise. There are literally hundreds of golf courses in the country, some of them designed by luminaries like Ronald Fream, Jack Nicklaus and Robert Trent Jones. There are over 50 courses alone within an easy hour's drive from Kuala Lumpur. Some of these courses

Above: Malaysia is often called a golfer's paradise

practical information

also offer night golfing under floodlights.

Close to the city is the famed **Royal Selangor Golf Club** (tel: 03-984 8433) off Jalan Tun Razak. Also fairly close to the city is the **Saujana Golf and Country Club** (tel:03- 746 1466) located near the Subang Airport, with a 36-hole golf course. Other clubs in the vicinity include the **Sultan Salahuddin Golf Club** (tel: 03-550 5872), **Glenmarie Golf and Country Club** (tel: 03-703 9090), both in Shah Alam. The Sultan Salahuddin also offers facilities for night golfing as well.

Further from KL is the **Rahman Putra Golf and Country Club** in Sungai Buloh (tel: 03-656 6870); **Templer Golf and Country Club** in Rawang (tel: 03-691 9617); **Awana Golf Club** in Genting Highlands (tel: 03-211 3015); and **Morib Golf Club** (tel: 03-858 1418).

Most clubs charge green fees for non-members. Further details may be obtained from the Malaysian Golfing Association, 12A, Persiaran Ampang, tel: 03-457 7931.

LANGUAGE

The Malay language, or Bahasa Malaysia, is polysyllabic, with variations in syllables to convey changes in meaning, unlike tonal languages such as Mandarin, Cantonese and Thai. For example, *duduk* (sit) is a verb. By adding the prefix *ke* and suffix *an*, we get the noun *kedudukan*, which means position. By adding a different prefix, *pen*, we get another noun, *penduduk*, which means inhabitant. Adding an *i* after *duduk* turns it into an active verb (to sit), while *menduduki* is a present continuous verb.

Tones do not vary to give different meanings and, for the most part, words are pronounced as they are spelt. In general, the pronunciation is the same as in English, with a few exceptions.

In Bahasa Malaysia, 'a' is pronounced 'ar' as in tar. The letter 'e' has an 'er' sound, as in reserve. You will also find that 'c' is pronounced 'ch' as in chair; the letter 'g' is always hard, as in gun and garden, not as in ginger; and 'sy' is pronounced 'sh'.

The language uses two distinct scripts: *Jawi* and *Rumi*. *Jawi* is the Arabic form of writing; *Rumi* the Roman alphabet, considered the easier of the two and also the official script of the country.

Here is a small vocabulary to get you on your way.

Numbers

1	Satu
2	Dua
3	Tiga
4	Empat
5	Lima
6	Enam
7	Tujuh
8	Lapan
9	Sembilan
10	Sepuluh
11	Sebelas
12	Dua belas
13	Tiga belas
20	Dua puluh
21	Dua puluh satu
100	Seratus
1,000	Seribu

Greetings and Others

How do you do?	Apa khabar?
Good morning	Selamat pagi
Good afternoon	Selamat petang
Good evening	Selamat malam
Goodbye	Selamat tinggal
Bon voyage	Selamat jalan
Fine/good	Baik
Thank you	Terima kasih
Please	Tolong/sila
Excuse me	Maafkan saya
I am sorry	Saya minta maaf
You're welcome	Sama-sama
My name is...	Nama saya...
Yes	Ya
No	Tidak

Pronouns

I	Saya
You	Anda/awak
He/she	Dia
We	Kami
They	Mereka

Forms of Address

Mr	Encik
Mrs	Puan
Miss	Cik

Directions and Travel

Where	*Di mana*
Right	*Kanan*
Left	*Kiri*
Turn	*Belok*
Go	*Pergi*
Stop	*Berhenti*
Follow	*Ikut*
Near	*Dekat*
Far	*Jauh*
Inside	*Dalam*
Outside	*Luar*
Front	*Hadapan*
Behind	*Belakang*
Here	*Sini*
There	*Sana*
Road	*Jalan*
Street	*Jalan*
Lane	*Lorong*
Bridge	*Jambatan*
Junction	*Simpang*
North	*Utara*
South	*Selatan*
East	*Timur*
West	*Barat*

Useful Phrases

How much?	*Berapa harganya?*
Can you help me?	*Bolehkah encik tolong saya?*
Where is this place?	*Di mana tempat ini?*
How far?	*Berapa jauh?*
I want to go to…	*Saya hendak pergi ke…*
Stop here	*Tolong berhenti sini*
Expensive	*Mahal*
Lower the price	*Kurangkan harganya*
Too big	*Besar sangat*
Too small	*Kecil sangat*
Any other colour?	*Ada warna lain?*

Other Handy Words

Drink	*Minum* (verb), *Minuman* (noun)
Eat	*Makan* (verb), *Makanan* (noun)
Fruit	*Buah-buahan*
Water	*Air*
Have	*Ada*
Don't have	*Tidak ada*
Toilet	*Tandas*
Why?	*Mengapa?*

When?	*Bila?*
Hot (spicy)	*Pedas*
Hot (heat)	*Panas*
Cold	*Sejuk*
Sweet	*Manis*
Sour	*Masam*
Delicious	*Sedap*
Clean	*Bersih*
Dirty	*Kotor*
Beautiful	*Cantik*
Open	*Buka*
Close	*Tutup*
Never	*Tidak pernah*
Often	*Selalu*
Sometimes	*Kadang-kadang*

USEFUL ADDRESSES

Tourist Offices

Tourism Malaysia
Level 2, 24–27th and 30th floor
Putra World Trade Centre
Jalan Tun Ismail
Tel: 03-293 5188
Email: tourism@tourism.gov.my
Website: www.tourism.gov.my

Malaysia Tourist Information Complex (MATIC)
109 Jalan Ampang
Tel: 03-264 3929
MATIC staff are knowledgeable and extremely helpful with tourist enquiries.

Tourism Malaysia Information Centres are also found at: Dataran Merdeka (underground), tel: 03-293 6664; Kuala Lumpur Railway Station, tel: 03-274 6063, KLIA (arrival hall), tel: 03-8787 4212.

Credit Card Offices

American Express
5th floor, Bangunan mas
Jalan Sultan Ismail
Tel: 03-261 4000
Open: Monday to Friday 8.30am–6pm; Saturday 8.30am–noon.

Diner's Club
Wisma Tan and Tan, Jalan Tun Razak
Tel: 03-261 1322, 261 1055
Email: diners@po.jaring.my

Right: window watchers

Open: Monday to Friday 9am–5pm; Saturday 9am–1pm.

MBF Mastercard Services
12th floor, Wisma MCA, Jalan Ampang
Tel: 03-262 2222
Open: Monday to Friday 9am–5pm; Saturday 9am–1pm.

FURTHER READING

Most bookshops carry a mediocre range of titles, with perhaps the exceptions being the University of Malaya's bookshop and Skoobs in Brickfields.

Major bookstores include the Berita Book Centre in Bukit Bintang Plaza, Times Distributors with branches in Sungei Wang Plaza and the Weld, MPH in Bangsar and Jaya's, Petaling Jaya, as well as Popular bookstores in Atrium and Jalan Petaling. The titles listed here are only a selection of the publications available in Malaysia.

Adoi, by Lee Kit, Times Books Intl, Singapore/Kuala Lumpur, 1989. A humourous, well-illustrated satire of Malaysian foibles and fancies.

Beaches of Malaysia, The Department of Irrigation and Drainage, Malaysia and Design Dimension Sdn Bhd, 1997. The first comprehensive photographic record of more than 168 beaches in Malaysia.

Chinatown, Kuala Lumpur, by Steve Bristow, and Edwin Lee, Tropical Press, Kuala Lumpur, 1994. Excellent photographs and history of Chinatown.

Culture Shock! Malaysia and Singapore, by Jo-Ann Craig, Times Books Intl. Interesting notes on the country's customs.

Insight Guide Malaysia, Apa Publications, Singapore, 1999. Best-selling book retains the basic structure of the original book published in 1985, with scores of new photographs and updated text.

Kuala Lumpur – A Sketchbook, by Chin Kon Yit and Chen Voon Fee, Archipelago Press, Singapore, 1998. Beautiful watercolour paintings of old Kuala Lumpur with suitably brief captions.

Maugham's Malaysian Stories, by Somerset Maugham, 1993, reprinted 1986. Masterful story-telling of British colonial life.

The Crafts of Malaysia, Dato' Haji Sulaiman Othman, Yeoh Jin Leng, etc, Archipelago Press, Singapore, 1994. A beautiful documentary of the development of the Malay arts in a changing society, with pictures of the best craft from museums.

The Food of Malaysia, edited by Wendy Hutton, Periplus Editions, Singapore, 1995. Handy-sized collection of local recipes with useful background information and lovely colour photographs.

The Malayan Trilogy, by Anthony Burgess, Penguin Books, London. Burgess' famous novel on post-war Malaya during the chaotic upheaval of independence.

The Malay Archipelago, by Alfred Russell Wallace, Graham Brash, Singapore, 1987. Wallace's famous account of his travels in the region. While in the East, Wallace formulated the theory of natural evolution, only to find that his contemporary Darwin had beaten him to the press.

The Malays – A Cultural History, by Richard Winstedt, revised and updated by Tham Seong Chee, Graham Brash, Singapore, 1981. A fascinating documentation of the Malays from pre-history to present day.

Turtle Beach, by Blanche d'Alpuget, Penguin 1981. Award-winning Australian novel on the plight of the Vietnamese people and their arrival in Malaysia.

practical information

INSIGHT
Pocket Guides

Insight Pocket Guides pioneered a new approach to guidebooks, introducing the concept of the authors as "local hosts" who would provide readers with personal recommendations, just as they would give honest advice to a friend who came to stay. They also included a full-size pull-out map. Now, to cope with the needs of the 21st century, new editions in this growing series are being given a new look to make them more practical to use, and restaurant and hotel listings have been greatly expanded.

c
r
e
d
i
t
s

ACKNOWLEDGEMENTS

Cover	**Telegraph Colour Library**
Backcover	**Arthur Teng**
Photography	**Ingo Jezierski/Apa Photo and**
Pages 15T, 25B, 50	**Axiom**
8/9, 42, 61T, 87	**Goh Seng Cheng**
10,11	**Mary Evans Picture Library**
5, 6B, 54, 55, 56	**R. Mohd. Noh**
12T	**Muzium Negara, Malaysia**
1, 15B, 28T, 45T/B, 91	**Christine Osborne**
59, 68	**Photobank Singapore**
13	**Picture Library/KL**
12B	**private archives**
14	**Paul Quayle**
2/3, 16, 24	**Chris Stowers/Panos Pictures**
21, 22, 29, 30, 31, 33T/B, 37, 38, 40, 43, 48, 51, 57, 60, 63, 64, 66, 70, 73, 76, 77, 78, 79, 85	**Arthur Teng**

Cartography	**Berndston & Berndston**
Cover Design	**Carlotta Junger**
Production	**Tanvir Virdee/Caroline Low**

INDEX